# LOVE'S LABOUR'S FOUND

*Shakespeare's Criminal Passions*

Stewart Trotter

Published by
Geerings
of Ashford Ltd.

ISBN No. 1 873953 35 6

***Cover photographs:***

William Shakespeare attributed to John Taylor.
*By courtesy of the National Portrait Gallery, London.*
William Shakespeare's handwriting, *Public Records Office.*
Henry Wriothesley, 3rd Earl of Southampton by unknown artist.
*Private collection on loan to the National Portrait Gallery, London.*

Published by Geerings of Ashford Ltd.

Printed by Geerings of Ashford Ltd., Cobbs Wood House, Chart Road, Ashford, Kent TN23 1EP. Telephone 01233 633366. Email: books@geerings.co.uk.

*For Amy*

# ACKNOWLEDGEMENTS

Thanks to my mentor and friend, C.C. Sheldrake, for discussing the ideas in this book with me; Jane Howell, Gaynor Miles, Catherine Fuller and Mike Burnside for travelling down to Titchfield to read 'Love's Labour's Lost'; Adolf Wood, Claire Lister, Jenny Sprince, Frank Dunlop and Barry Shaw for reading through a draft of this book and giving me their help and advice; John Lyall, for his architectural insights; Michael Jackson for combing through the text; the Librarians and Staff of the Winchester Record Office, the Thomas Plume Library at Maldon, the British Library, the Public Record Office at Kew and the London Library, for their meticulous assistance; Prof. Andrew Sanders for his encouragement; my agent Kevin Fraser for his belief and support and Robert Geering for publishing the book. Also to my daughter, Amy, without whose gentle curiosity, patience and love this study might never have been undertaken. And certainly never finished.

S.T.

# CONTENTS

# PRELUDE

If you click the name of 'William Shakespeare' on the Internet, you will find 'The Earl of Oxford' in the first six hits. Many otherwise sane, intelligent people believe that Oxford was the true author of the plays attributed to Shakespeare.

How, they argue, could the son of an illiterate tradesman from Stratford-upon-Avon display an intimate knowledge of high Tudor politics, history, philosophy, classics, Italian culture and French Renaissance thought?

How could he acquire his massive vocabulary? Come to that, how could he buy the books, paper, pen and ink to write his plays?

Following a hunch and a picnic with my daughter, I believe I have the answer....

# CHAPTER 1

## SITTING IN THE SKY

At the beginning of Shakespeare's early comedy, 'Love's Labour's Lost', Don Adriano de Armado, a fantastical Spaniard, writes an outraged letter to the King of Navarre. Costard the swain and Jaquenetta the country wench have been copulating in the King's own Park:

'The place where? It standeth north-north-east and by east from the west corner of thy curious knotted garden'.

Later the Princess of France, visiting the King on state business, asks:

> Was that the king that spurr'd his horse so hard
> Against the steep-uprising of the hill?

I have directed 'Love's Labour's Lost' twice, once in Clare Gardens as a Cambridge undergraduate and once as Artistic Director of the Northcott Theatre in Devon. Both times I had a feeling that Shakespeare was writing about a real place. But where?

Shakespeare dedicated his poems 'Venus and Adonis' and 'The Rape of Lucrece' to Henry Wriothesley ('Harry Southampton') the young 3rd Earl of Southampton and Baron of Titchfield. The obvious place to start was his country estate - if it was still there. I phoned the Hampshire Tourist Board: 'Yes, the ruins of Titchfield Abbey were still standing – but no, there was no garden. The locals burn an effigy of the 3rd Earl each year because he built a sea-wall which cut off the river to the town. They also believe that Shakespeare wrote 'Romeo and Juliet' at Titchfield – a lot of nonsense of course...'

That was enough for me to pack a picnic hamper and

persuade my teenage daughter Amy that a Whitsun outing to Titchfield Abbey was worth it. Secretly I feared we would find a super-market car-park. On the train down to the South Coast we skimmed the tourist bumph:

'In 1232 Henry III granted the estate of Titchfield to the Premonstratensians, a French, white-robed, order of monks. Because ships at that time could sail round the Isle of Wight right up to Titchfield Harbour, it became an important embarkation point for France. Henry V stayed there in 1415 before setting off with his army for Agincourt and Henry VI married Margaret of Anjou in the Abbey Church in 1445. On his break with Rome, Henry VIII dissolved the monastery in 1537 and gave it to Thomas Wriothesley (1505-1550), later 1st Earl of Southampton, who converted it into 'a right stately house' called 'The Place'. The 2nd Earl (1545-1581), his son, was imprisoned in the Tower of London for political activity. The 3rd Earl (1573-1624) was patron to several writers, including William Shakespeare. The line died out with the 4th Earl'.

The taxi from Fareham swung past 'The Mill' pub into the magnificent ruins of the Abbey. True, there was no garden. But I looked down in amazement at an overgrown, sunken patch of ground, grass waist-high, that would have once made a perfect knot-garden, a Tudor creation of inter-woven flower beds. A beaten path through the grass led to a picnic table that seemed to be waiting for us.

I climbed into a stunted apple tree and, to my daughter's embarrassment, declaimed some lines from the play:

> Like a demi-God, here sit I in the sky,
> And wretched fools' secrets heedfully o'er-eye.
> More sacks to the mill! O heavens I have my wish;
> Dumaine transformed: four woodcocks in a dish.

'More sacks to the mill'. Could that be the Mill pub we had just passed in the taxi?

I turned to the songs of Spring and Winter that end the play. Could all the people mentioned, Tom, who 'bears logs into the hall', Dick the shepherd who 'blows his nail', Marian whose 'nose looks red and raw' and 'greasy Joan' who keels the pot all be people who once lived and worked in this great household? I noticed a line in the Spring Song: 'And maidens bleach their summer smocks'. The night before our Titchfield trip, Amy had spilt coffee over her white summer dress. It had spent the night in very non-Tudor bleach. The spirits of the household seemed to be joking with us. Not sure if I was in the 1590's or the present, in a garden or a set, in life or in a play, I packed the picnic hamper. As I was leaving the Abbey, something made me look round. There, beyond the garden wall, was 'the steep-uprising of the hill...'

Amy and I walked down to Titchfield town, picking wild flowers on the way. Were they the 'lady-smocks all silver white' or 'cuckoo buds of yellow hue' mentioned in the song? We were so happily pre-occupied we walked right past the answer to the play's greatest puzzle.

●

I now needed the help of friends. How did the play feel read aloud at Titchfield Abbey? A few weeks later a gypsy band of directors, actors (and my ever-loyal daughter) boarded the Waterloo train again, laden down with picnic baskets, Panama hats, sun cream and scripts. We sat at the picnic table, shared our food and wine, and read the whole play.

The plot is a simple one. The King of Navarre and three young Lords, Berowne, Longaville and Dumaine, having vowed to retire from the world to study for three years, fall, one by one, for the visiting Princess of France and her Ladies-in-Waiting, Rosaline, Maria and Katharine. But the language, thought and texture of the play are of a dazzling, complex, richness. They are similar to Shakespeare's Sonnets, written for his 'private friends': and, like them, lead directly to Shakespeare's heart.

We found 'Love's Labour's Lost' an ideal play for the open air. On arriving from France, the Princess complains to the King that 'the roof of this court is too high to be yours, and welcome to the wide fields too base to be mine'. All the action takes place in a park before the doors of a Manor House. There are references to the 'grass' beneath the players' feet and the 'leaves' of the bushes where the Lords hide their illicit love poems. A play of early summer, it mentions flowers of spring (columbines, daisies, violets) 'green geese' (the first grass-fed geese to be eaten in the year) and 'Love whose month is ever May'. At one point the flamboyant factotum, Boyet, tells the Ladies to 'Blow like sweet roses in this summer air.' The play's light beauty was an ideal compliment to 'Place House' and its grounds. In Shakespeare's time, when the Princess and her Ladies arrive from France, they could have landed by water at Titchfield itself.

But the play is also full of mystery. Why does Shakespeare, in what the first printing describes as a 'pleasant conceited comedy', deal with such profound subjects as perjury, guilt and man's aching need for forgiveness? And why does it end, not with the resolution of the marriage-bed, but the death of the King of France?

The day after the picnic, I began research - I was going to say 'in earnest' but it was so enjoyable – at the Winchester Record Office. I was well aware that my 'knot-garden' might turn out to be a 1930's roller-skating rink, 'The Mill' part of a 1970's restaurant chain. I was in luck: the Record Office had a Victorian copy of an early Jacobean map of Titchfield. There, clearly labelled, were 'The Parke' and 'The Place' both mentioned in Don Armado's letter. There was the mill by the river. I also found early eighteenth century plans of the house marking steps to 'the Parterre'- exactly where I thought the knot-garden had been.

As I studied the play it threw up more and more conundrums. I believe I have solved them. And I believe I have uncovered the politically explosive, erotically charged and dangerously subversive circumstances of its first production. I have also discovered where Shakespeare spent his 'lost years'. And how he *really* fell in love.

To understand Shakespeare we must first understand his 'secret' family, the completely dysfunctional, profoundly Catholic and suicidally rebellious Southamptons. They were to inform all of Shakespeare's plays – and all of Shakespeare's life.

# CHAPTER 2.

# TOWERS AND BATTLEMENTS

Thomas Wriothesley, Harry Southampton's grandfather, was a civilised brute with a taste for racking women and burning them to death. Real name 'Writh', son of a Court official[*] and drinking-companion to Henry VIII, he shared at least one characteristic with the King. Neither of the Abbots of Titchfield nor Beaulieu, when they surrendered their run-down Abbeys to Wriothesley, possessed a horse big enough to carry him.

When Henry, desperate for a son, broke with Rome so that he could divorce Katharine of Arragon and marry Anne Boleyn, he ordered the destruction of all Catholic icons – including beloved images of the Virgin Mary holding the baby Jesus. Wriothesley (rhyming with grisly) smashed up the Hampshire tombs of St. Swithin and Alfred the Great. He then went on to smash up the Chapel of Titchfield Abbey itself to create a master-bedroom. His wife, Jane, though, like the vast majority of Tudor aristocrats, remained devoutly Catholic all her life. Her horror at the destruction of the Abbey Church was placated by her husband's plans to turn the Chapter House into a private chapel where the old Latin Mass was said, and the Virgin Mary worshipped, way into the reign of Elizabeth – and possibly beyond. Possessing a copy of the Works of Chaucer, inscribed at several points with her name, Jane Southampton was lively, accomplished, popular and iron-willed.

'My mistress is in good health and is most kind to Mrs. Russhe and me' wrote Wriothesley's servant to his master on 1st February, 1538. 'She also handleth the country gentlemen, the farmers and their wives to your great worship and every night is

---

[*] A 'Garter King of Arms' in charge of granting family crests.

as merry as can be with Christmas plays and masques with Anthony Gedge and other of your servants'.

Wriothesley literally turned his home into a castle by adding illegal 'towers and battlements'. Henry forgave him and made him Baron of Titchfield. But Wriothesley had laid up a curse for his descendants. A fort, by a navigable river, on the south coast facing Europe, was a threat to 'the State'. 'The State', a handful of ruthless, driven people, was over the years to take its revenge. But 'The Place' was a blessing too. It gave the members of its household, led for the most part by women, the wherewithal to examine themselves, encourage others, and try to work their will upon the world.

Wriothesley worked his too hard. At the Coronation of King Henry's son, the fanatically Protestant boy-king, Edward VI, Wriothesley insisted on carrying the Sword of State, semaphoring his intention to run England. Others had the same idea. Wriothesley was created 1st Earl of Southampton in February, 1547, but sacked as Lord Chancellor a month later. He plotted, was plotted against, and died, dropped, in 1550, at the age of 45. But like his beloved King Henry, whose death he reported to Parliament in tears, he was attractive when young. John Leland (c.1506-1552), a Cambridge friend, described how he looked when he appeared in a College play:

'Your beauty so shone upon your brow, your head of golden hair so glistened, the light of your keen mind was so effulgent, and your winning virtue so adorned you, that, one amongst many*, you were seen to be a pattern for all'.

Most important of all, he had a good ear for music.

His only surviving son, Henry, (whose godparents were Henry VIII and his daughter Mary Tudor) inherited his title as 2nd Earl of Southampton, at the age of five. Defying young King

---

* 'Ung par tout – tout par ung' - *One for all, all for one* - was the Wriothesley family motto.

Edward's hatred of Papism – with its relics, processions and prayers for the dead - Jane Southampton brought up her son and her five daughters as strict Catholics. She ran the family, and the vast Titchfield household and estates, till her son's marriage fifteen years later. Edward himself called at Titchfield in 1552, the year before his early death. Jane's candles, rosaries and statues must have been hurriedly packed away. A year later, with Catholic 'Bloody' Mary's Accession, out they came again. Jane even rode in a carriage in the Queen's procession. But back they finally went with Elizabeth, whose first act as monarch in 1558 was to ban the Elevation of the Host at the Communion Service.

The rise and rise of the violently anti-Papist, William Cecil (1521-1589), later Lord Burghley, and his round-backed son, Sir Robert Cecil (1563-1612), made life a growing nightmare for Jane and all members of the 'Old Faith'. Elizabeth, who installed herself as Head of the Church like her father Henry VIII, claimed she had no window to see into men's souls. But with Burghley and Sir Robert around, plus their co-opted network of neighbourhood spies, she frankly did not need one.

Jane was so alienated from this Protestant establishment that in December, 1564 the Privy Council actually had to order her and her son, the nineteen year old 2nd Earl (still living with his mother in Titchfield), 'in her Highness name' to attend the Christmas court 'without further delay or protract of time'. Two years later the 2nd Earl flaunted his religion by marrying into one of the oldest Catholic families in the land, the Brownes of Cowdray Castle, twenty miles away from Titchfield. The beautiful, spirited Mary Browne, daughter of Viscount Montague, became his teenage bride in 1566. Mother Jane did not approve. Perhaps she knew Mary, a girl brought up by a step-mother with five children of her own, would prove as stubborn as her son. Or perhaps, lacking a husband, she just wanted to keep the 2nd Earl for herself.

Three years later, on 3rd August, 1569, Queen Elizabeth dined with her relation, the 4th Duke of Norfolk, at nearby Farnham. Her double-dealing lover, Robert Dudley, the Earl of Leicester, was expected there as well, but sent to say he was at death's door, nursed by his 'cousins' at Titchfield. Norfolk, who claimed to be a Protestant, admitted to the Queen at lunch that he intended to marry the widowed Mary, Queen of Scots. Elizabeth, suspecting 'gypsy' Leicester's connivance, stormed over to Titchfield and, hauling him into the gallery of 'The Place', 'roundly reprimanded him for attempting a match with the Queen of Scots without her cognisance'.

The Earl of Sussex, the 2nd Earl's brother-in-law, who was staying at 'Place House" at the time, also fell under suspicion. Burghley entered in his Diary: 'I wrote to the Earl of Sussex, to know what had passed from him in the matter of the Duke of Norfolk, at Titchfield, Southampton.' He thought that Sussex was at the centre of a Titchfield plot.

He was right. The 2nd Earl of Southampton and his father-in-law Lord Montague, egged on by old Jane Southampton, were working with their Catholic relations, the Northern Lords, to place Mary, Queen of Scots, on the throne of England. The next month, with a celebration of the Old Mass at Durham Cathedral, the ill-fated Rebellion went ahead. Elizabeth, with a canny, divisive stroke, ordered the Earl of Sussex to put it down. Eight hundred men, including the Earl of Northumberland, and ultimately the Duke of Norfolk, were executed. Some of the Northern Lords claimed they were trying to counter the anti-Catholic influence of Burghley. Others, that they were trying to safeguard the Succession. But as Elizabeth remarked, to recognise Mary as her heir 'would be to spread my own winding-sheet before my eyes'.

The 2nd Earl and Montague sailed towards Europe to join forces with the Catholic Duke of Alba. Winds blew them back to England and the Queen. Elizabeth 'forgave' Montague, and, showing that loyalty to her brought its rewards, made him Lord Lieutenant – the Queen's representative in his Shire. Montague was later to demonstrate his loyalty, if not his conversion, by raising a private army to fight the Armada. But the unrepentantly Papist 2nd Earl, placed under house arrest with a Protestant family in Guildford, was compelled to celebrate the Cranmer English Communion Service, a beautifully written State fudge designed to accommodate Catholic and Anglican alike.

In the following year, 1570, Pope Pius V, an austere, remote Dominican friar, issued his devastating Papal Bull. He excommunicated Queen Elizabeth, invited Catholics to assassinate her and vetoed the new English Mass. At a stroke he made it impossible for an Englishman to be both a devout Catholic and a loyal subject.

The 2nd Earl, fearing for his soul, arranged a night meeting in the Lambeth marshes with the Bishop of Ross, agent to Mary, Queen of Scots. Was it right for him, as a Catholic, to obey Elizabeth? He told the Bishop he would prefer to 'lose all that he had' than be troubled by 'a continual fear of conscience.' Ross, under torture, betrayed the Earl, who was imprisoned in the Tower from October, 1571 to May, 1573. Mary Southampton must have had visiting rights. The 3rd Earl, Harry Southampton, Shakespeare's patron, and little brother to his sister Mary, was born on 6th October, 1573.

Jane Southampton, who died the following year, had been right about the marriage. Her son and Mary grew to loathe each other. The 2nd Earl, worked on by a family 'friend', aided by a gentleman of the bed-chamber, Thomas Dymock, accused her of adultery with 'a common person'. This charge Mary refuted all her life: but the 2nd Earl broke off all relations both with his wife and her family, the Montague/Brownes.

In a sad letter to her father Lord Montague, Mary describes how she is 'condemned generally, though I trust not so much of the better sort that knoweth me'. She prophesies that her husband 'will mix up old matters, repented and forgotten long since' but, asserting her innocence, says 'he may blame me of folly, but never justly condemn me of fault'. This is a Catholic woman, aware of her soul, writing in confession to her Catholic father. She had clearly fallen in love with the 'common person' (her 'folly') but there is no reason to doubt her assertion she never committed the 'fault' of sleeping with him. She adds an extraordinary P.S.: 'That your Lordship shall be witness of my desire to win my Lord by all such means as resteth in me, I have sent you what I sent him [a letter which has been lost] by my little boy. But his heart was too great to bestow the reading of it coming from me. Yet will I do my part so long as I am with him, but good my Lord, procure so soon as conveniently you may some end to my misery, for I am tired with this life.'

Thus she turns her father into her lover, and her six year old son into a postman. The 2nd Earl's heart was indeed so 'great' with this brazen abuse of his son that he determined Mary would never see young Harry again. For the two years before his death he succeeded, filling his son's own heart with an uncompromising love of Catholicism and an uncompromising hatred of women. He retreated behind 'a whole troupe of of at least a hundred well-mounted gentlemen and yeomen' and 'tall goodly fellows that kept a constant pace'. He would only communicate with his wife through Dymock, upon whom he grew increasingly dependent. As Mary had observed: 'This house is not for them who will not honour Dymock as a God'.

Faith was the final undoing of the 2nd Earl. In 1580 the Jesuits sent Edmund Campion – a charismatic Oxford priest who had defected to Rome – back to England on a suicide mission to recall Elizabeth and her subjects to the Old Faith. Arrested, and racked so savagely he lost the use of his arm, Campion revealed how a complex network of recusants, of all classes and walks of life, including Dymock, had planned a meeting between himself and the 2nd Earl.* On the same day the Privy Council resolved to 'examine' the Earl 'what Jesuits or Priests he hath known, where they have been harboured and by whom relieved, what letters or messages he hath received or sent unto them, and where they remain'.

Whether they did 'examine' or imprison him we do not know. But two months later, at the age of 36, he was dead.

He despised his wife to the end. His will places Dymock in charge not only of his estates but of his son Harry as well. He even forbade his only daughter Mary, on pain of losing her inheritance, to live in the same house as her mother. Contemptuous of a will which made 'his servant his wife', Mary reversed it. Pulling family strings with Leicester, she made sure it was one of her own men, not Dymock ('void of either wit, ability or honesty') who administered the estates. In a stunning burst of honesty she declares 'that his Lordship continued his hard mind towards me to his last, I grieve more for his soul than any harm he hath done therein, for my assurance of living rested not in his arms to bear. For the rest I weigh not, but by my troth am rather glad he hath given me so just a cause to forget him that otherwise I should have carried my remembrance with grief more than enough to my last hour.'

Her daughter, on orders of Queen Elizabeth, was returned to

---

* 'He (Campion) had delivered a copy of his 'Challenge' to one Norice, a priest commonly remaining about London, that he deliver it to one Pounde, then prisoner in the Marshalsea, who is thought to have dispersed the same abroad, and that one Stephens brought the said Pound to speak with Campion at Throgmorton House in London. Further that Pound directed Campion by a token to one Dymock to speak with the Earl of Southampton'. Acts of the Privy Council, (4th August, 1581)

her two days before her husband's funeral. Harry Southampton, eight when his father died and equally self-willed, refused to attend any Anglican service. Lord Burghley snatched him away from the nest of Titchfield Catholics, made him a Ward of Court, educated him at his own home in London and at Cambridge University, and tried to turn him into a Protestant. Straight after Harry's sixteenth birthday in 1589, Burghley also tried to turn him into a relation. He ordered him to marry his Protestant granddaughter, Elizabeth de Vere, and gave him a year 'to decide'. Harry, back at Titchfield, would have none of it. Like his father, he now preferred the company of men.

One of them was the dashing young Robert Devereaux, 2nd Earl of Essex, (1566-1601) another of Burghley's wards, and seven years older than himself, a hero. When, in 1591, Essex went to fight the Catholics in France alongside King Henri of Navarre, Harry begged Elizabeth to be allowed to join him. She refused, ostensibly on the grounds of his age, but really because she knew that the two young men together spelt trouble. Besides, she wanted the whole of Essex's attention. And the whole of Sir Walter Raleigh's as well...

Her beloved Leicester had died three years earlier at 55 and Elizabeth – who liked to lounge back on cushions while her courtiers knelt formally before her - needed a replacement favourite. She had set up Essex and Raleigh as rivals and, naturally enough, the proud young Lord in his early 20's and the brilliant, devious Devonian, fourteen years his senior, had grown to detest each other. They had even exchanged blows. Now Essex was away at Rouen, Raleigh had every opportunity to bad-mouth him to his Queen.

The politics of 1591 were further complicated by one of Elizabeth's sinister summer 'Progresses' to the South East of England.

# CHAPTER 3.

# ELISA, QUEEN OF SECOND TROY

On the face of it, a Progress was the Queen's gracious response to an invitation from one of her subjects to 'come and stay'. Leaving her Richmond Palace – and its stinking summer privies – Elizabeth would often arrive with her entire court. Her hosts, with masques, music, dancing and feasts, would celebrate this self-styled Cynthia, Diana, Moon-Goddess and Fairy Queen. Elizabeth visited the old Lord Montague, Harry Southampton's grandfather, at Cowdray in August, 1591. So desperate was he to prove his loyalty, he had an account of his entertainment set up in print before it had even finished.

On Saturday, 15th, at 8 p.m., the pamphlet tells us, Elizabeth arrived 'with a great a train'. As soon as she was spotted, musicians struck up; but when she reached the bridge before Cowdray Castle, the music suddenly cut out. In the dramatic silence a porter in armour confronted her with a wooden club and a golden key. Cowdray, he claimed, was a second Thebes whose walls could only keep standing as long as music played. Now, with the arrival of Elizabeth, music is no longer needed. An ancient prophesy predicted that the 'walls should shake and the roof totter, till the wisest, and fairest, and most fortunate of all creatures, should by her first step make the foundation staid, and by the glance of her eyes make the turret steady'. The Porter hails Elizabeth as the 'miracle of Time, Nature's glory, Fortune's Empress, the world's wonder'.

Fairy-tales over, he cuts to politics. He assures the Queen that Lord Montague's 'tongue is the key of his heart: and his heart the lock of his soul. Therefore what he speaks you may constantly believe: which is, that in duty and service to your

Majesty he would be second to none: in praying for your happiness, equal to any'. Decoded, Montague is saying to Elizabeth: 'I am a Catholic, but I have not utterly followed the Papal Bull which orders Catholics to withdraw their loyalty from you – and then kill you. I do, however, constantly pray for your conversion to Rome, which would make you happy in this world and the next.'

The Porter then presents Elizabeth with the key to Cowdray, the key to his Master's heart. Taking it, she replies 'She would swear for him there was none more faithful'. Whether she means 'faithful to her', or 'faithful to Rome' is left hanging in the air.

Alighting from her horse, Elizabeth embraces the Lady Montague, who, in a well-scripted response, 'as it were weeping in her bosom' exclaims 'Oh happy time, oh joyful day'. What the pamphlet does not record is a full meeting of the Anti-Papist Privy Council that very evening in Montague's vacated house.

The next day was Sunday. No Divine Worship, in public at least, is recorded. Lord Montague roasted 'three oxen and one hundred and forty geese' for what one can only hope was a late 'breakfast'. At eight next morning the Queen rode 'with all her train' to the park where a 'delicate bower' had been prepared to house 'her Highnesse musicians'. A nymph handed Elizabeth a crossbow and sang a 'sweet song':

> Goddess and Monarch of this happy Isle,
>> Vouchsafe this bow which is an huntress part;
> Your eyes are arrows though they seem to smile
>> Which never glanced but galled the stateliest hart,
> Strike one, strike all, for none at all can fly,
>> They gaze you in the face although they die.

'Strike one, strike all' is another reference to the Wriothesley family motto – 'All for one, one for all' – so Harry Southampton,

Montague's grandson, must have been in attendance. The 'stately' teenager, with a play on 'hart' and 'heart', is being offered up by his family to Elizabeth as her next favourite, slain, like the deer, by the Queen's beauty. He was probably instructed to kneel and gaze rapturously at her face.

Seated in a specially erected 'standing', the Queen then took pot-shots at thirty rounded-up deer that were run before her between nets. Her father had initiated this degraded form of hunting, loathed by country folk, when he became too fat and ill to mount a horse. To a musical accompaniment, the Queen slaughtered four deer and Montague's sister, Lady Kildare, in an effort to be diplomatic, just one. She was not invited to join the Queen's table at supper.

On Tuesday afternoon, viewing 'my Lord's walks', the Queen stumbled across a Pilgrim, 'clad in a coat of russet velvet…his hat being of the same, with scallop shells of cloth of silver'. Hailing the Queen as 'Fairest of all creatures' he tells her of a marvellous oak tree, hung with ornaments, guarded by a 'rough-hewed ruffian' with a stave. She follows him and finds the tree hung both with her own arms and the arms of all the 'Noblemen and Gentlemen of that Shire'. The wild man compares the mighty oak to Elizabeth, protected by her noblemen and gentlemen and by a sea 'rampired with true hearts'. Abroad the Queen's courage has made her feared: but at home it is her 'clemency' which 'the owner of this grove hath tasted' that has made her loved.

Thus Montague thanks Elizabeth for not chopping off his head after the Rebellion of the Northern Lords. That night, the Privy Council meets again.

On Wednesday Montague picnics his Queen *al fresco* at a table twenty-four yards long. Elizabeth encounters yet another allegorical figure, an Angler this time, fishing 'in a goodly fish-pond' who moralises on the fallen state of this 'nibbling' world. He blames his inability to catch even an oyster on the awesome presence of a Goddess: 'The sun so glisters that the fish see my hook through the bait'. At that moment a Fisherman appears, dragging nets filled with fish towards the Queen. He would have preferred to have caught all the 'hollow hearts' of the kingdom instead as there are some of Elizabeth's subjects 'so muddy-minded, that they cannot live in a clear river but a standing pool'. After much play on 'carp' and 'carping', 'perch' and 'perching for position', the Fisherman finally lands his nets and lays out the fish -'unworthy a present for a Prince to accept' – at the feet of the Queen.

On Thursday Elizabeth dines with all the neighbouring 'Lords and Ladies in the privy walks in the garden' at a table which has grown to forty-eight yards. In the evening the country people present themselves to Her Majesty 'in a pleasant dance with tabor and pipe: and the Lord Montague and his Lady among them, to the great pleasure of all the beholders, and gentle applause of her Majesty.'

●

The truth is 'The Fairy Queen', hitting 60, plastered with make-up and with cloth stuffed into her cheeks to fill them out, had invited herself to Cowdray. Surrounded by her Privy Council and its spies, she was forcing ritual obedience upon a Catholic family and, by casting herself as a Goddess, attempting to obliterate all memory of the Virgin Mary. On a Progress to Norfolk in 1578 she had actually arrested her hosts for their adherence to the Old Faith. She might not have been so eager to applaud the dancing of Lord and Lady Montague, however gently, if she had known then what the Privy Council was to discover two years later. Priests, ordained in Bloody Mary's time, were still resident at Cowdray and still celebrating the

Latin Mass. A recusant called Shelley 'used to carry priests, up and down with him' in Lord Montague's livery with 'chains of gold about their necks'. Catholic priests could well have served Queen Elizabeth her dinners at Cowdray. They would certainly have eaten the fish from the net, as a penance, on the Friday. Luckily old Lord Montague was dead when his servants were 'examined' by the Privy Council. Elizabeth, enigmatic as ever, had sat by his deathbed, feeding him soup from a spoon.

●

After the Cowdray Progress, Elizabeth paid an early September visit to Titchfield. A Privy Council meeting was held, Elizabeth slaughtered more deer from two 'standings' and doubtless Lord Harry's 'wedding plans' were discussed. Later that month, Elizabeth dropped in 'by chance' on Lord Hertford at Elvetham, twenty miles north of Titchfield. This was not the grandest of Hertford's estates; but he wanted to show his 'unfeigned love' and 'most loyal duty to her most gracious Highness'. So he employed three hundred men for weeks before her arrival to construct a complete town on a hillside in his park. There was a 'room of estate' for the nobles with a withdrawing room for the Queen. Accommodation was also provided for Her Majesty's footmen (and their friends), her Guard, the officers of her House and any 'commoners, suitors and such-like'. On the same hill kitchens, butteries, boiling houses, sculleries and accommodation for the cooks were also built. It was like feeding an army.

It *was* feeding an army. Elizabeth wanted to protect herself from others who fancied her job. In addition, between the hill and the Lord's house, in compliment to Elizabeth, workmen had dug a 'goodly pond cut to the perfect figure of a half-moon'.

Hertford, with three hundred of his men, wearing chains of gold round their necks and yellow and black feathers in their caps, rode to greet the Queen. A poem of welcome in Latin was recited; then six singing virgins strew flowers before this 'Queen of second Troy' as she entered her Fairy Palace.

The next morning, being England, it rained; but in the afternoon a green satin canopy, 'upheld by four of my Lord's chief gentlemen', was erected by the pond for the Queen to sit under. From a bower emerged a 'pompous array of sea-persons' (actors dressed as Tritons) who, plunging into the autumnal waters, waded or swam to the Queen. 'Cheerfully sounding their trumpets', they drew behind them a miniature galleon with 'three virgins, which, with their cornets, played Scottish jigs'. One of the Tritons did a somersault from the pinnace into the water. Then Nereus, a 'sea-prophet', presented to the Queen a fabulous jewel 'hidden in a purse of green rushes, cunningly woven together'. Sylvanus, no doubt played by a handsome, muscular young actor to please the Queen, emerged from the woods, dressed in kid's-skin breeches, his 'legs, body, and face naked but dyed over with saffron' and presented Elizabeth with a shield from the God Apollo. A battle ensues: Sylvanus and his followers throw darts and Nereus and his Tritons spray them with wooden water 'squirts'. Nereus finally calls for an end to the conflict 'grounded on the excellence of Her Majesty's presence, as being always friend to peace and enemy to war'. The Sylvans slink away. A sea-nymph presents Elizabeth with yet another costly 'sea-jewel', Elizabeth names the nymph's galleon 'The Bonadventure' and to the sound of trumpets, the aquatic ballet concludes. Elizabeth is so pleased she actually pays the actors.

The rest of the Progress entertainment includes a massive fire-work display and a great torch-lit procession of a thousand dishes of 'sugar work'. But on the fourth day something remarkable happens. A woman playing Aureola, Queen of the Fairies, appears at dawn, dancing beneath Elizabeth's casement window. Someone, it seems, is hinting that Elizabeth is not the true Fairy Queen....

On her departure 'in an extreme rain', the actors, in costume, lined her way, wringing their hands in sorrow at the loss of the sun from the land. It is unlikely that Lord Hertford, 'of very small stature and of timid and feeble character', shared this grief. In 1560 he had secretly married Lady Catherine Grey (sister of Lady Jane Grey) who, by the terms of Henry VIII's will, was next in line to the throne. In a fury Elizabeth had them both locked in the Tower for a couple of years. Then she put them under house arrest. Her anger cooled slightly when Catherine died: but she refused to acknowledge the legitimacy of the marriage, or of the son they had produced, Lord Beauchamp. This young Lord, with a claim to the throne of England much better than Elizabeth's, is notably absent from his father's 'celebrations'.

Given their cost, he would remain notably absent from the throne as well. When Elisa called, no-one had any money left to raise an army against her. She kept her subjects loyal by bankrupting them. And, failing that, there was always the Tower. Hertford was in it again five years later for trying to legitimise his son.

In October Elizabeth broke her Progress and returned to Richmond. She repaid her hosts' hospitality by appointing Commissioners for each Shire in England 'to enquire of all persons as to their attendance at Church, their receiving of seminarists, priests and Jesuits, their devotion to the Pope or King of Spain, and to give information as to suspicious changes of residence'. True to form, Raleigh called in at Richmond to report that Essex had been creating, illegally, scores of knights at Rouen.

●

Back at Titchfield the pressure on young Harry Southampton was mounting. Burghley was threatening a tremendous £5,000 fine (£2,5000,000 in today's money) if he did not marry his granddaughter. His mother Mary, still in control of the purse-strings, and his grandfather Montague had gone over to Burghley's side the previous year. To crown it all, a poet had bombarded him with seventeen sonnets on his seventeenth birthday – all trying to persuade him to marry.

The very first sonnet played on the family name:

> From fairest creatures we desire increase,
> That thereby beauty's *Rose* might never die*

In the third sonnet he flatters the boy's mother, Mary:

> Thou art thy mother's glass and she in thee
> Calls back the lovely April of her prime

*You are like your mother's looking glass: when she looks at you, you are like a reflection of her younger self.*

And in the thirteenth sonnet he mentions the dead 2nd Earl:

> You had a father; let your son say so.

How had a glover's son from Stratford-upon-Avon got mixed up in high Tudor politics in Hampshire?

---

* 'Wriothesley' could also be pronounced 'Rosely'. One of the family crests in the Hall of 'The Place' portrayed a rose. *Wriothesley Papers*, (Winchester Record Office).

# CHAPTER 4.

# THE BUTCHER'S BOY

For a start, William Shakespeare was 'related' to the Southamptons.

His mother Mary was a 'yeoman' Arden, born in Wilmcote in Warwickshire. The 'gentry' Park Hall Ardens lived twelve miles away: their Edward Arden was circuitously related, via Sir Henry Browne, to Mary Southampton. The precise nature of Mary's relationship to Edward has been debated. Edmond Malone (1741-1812), the Irish barrister and great Shakespearean scholar (in his unfinished 'Life of Shakespeare' published in 1821) thought Mary Arden was descended from Robert Arderne, brother of John Arderne – Squire for the Body to Henry VII.

Father H.S.Bowden, a Catholic priest writing in 1899, but basing his work on a manuscript by Richard Simpson written in the 1860's, thought she was related to another of John's brothers, Thomas.★

Mark Eccles, a modern scholar, states in 'Shakespeare in Warwickshire'(1961):'there is no proof that Shakespeare was related to the Ardens of Park Hall'. But he admits that 'it is possible that Thomas [Arden of Wilmcote, Shakespeare's grandfather] may have descended from a younger son of that family'.

The Tudors were less precise when claiming relationships. Malone tells us they loved to enlarge their families, more by

---

★ 'Edward Arden of Parkhall, not far from Snitterfield, … was married to Mary, daughter of Sir George and sister of Sir Robert Throckmorton of Coughton, and consequently aunt of Sir Robert's daughter, the wife of Sir William Catesby of Bushwood Park in Stratford. Anne, the daughter of Lady Catesby, was married to Sir Henry Browne, son of the first Lord Montague; and Sir Henry Browne's sister Mary was Countess of Southampton and mother of Henry, Earl of Southampton'. Fr. H.S.Bowden *The Religion of Shakespeare*, (1899).

'affinity' than 'consanguinity'. As the Catholic Countess says to the servant girl Helena in 'All's Well That Ends Well' as she 'adopts' her:

> 'Tis often seen
> Adoption strives with nature, and choice breeds
> A native slip to us from foreign seeds

*It is a common experience that an adopted child can be as loved as a natural one: when we choose who is to become part of our family, we are often drawn to them as one of our own, even though technically they are not of our blood.*

The very fact that Shakespeare's mother had the Arden name and was born so close to Park Hall, would be enough for Shakespeare to claim a relationship with the Southamptons. And claim it he did. When he came to apply for a Coat of Arms for his own family in 1596 it included 'a falcon his wings displayed Argent'. The Southampton family arms consist, as can be seen to this day on their tomb at St. Peter's Church in Titchfield, of 'Azure a Cross Or between four falcons argent'. In 1599 the Shakespeare family applied to add the Arden arms to their own – and in a cancelled draft the Herald actually drew in the arms of the Park Hall Ardens.

But why had Shakespeare linked himself to the Southamptons? And why had he left Stratford?

The answer lies in the fortunes of the Shakespeare family. We know from contemporary Stratford documents that William's father John, as well as being a glover, was a taster of ale and bread for the county, an assessor of fines, a constable, an alderman and in 1568 was elected Bailiff of Stratford, the town's highest office. Shakespeare was four at the time, so his father must have seemed a very impressive figure in his 'robes and furred gowns'. But in 1575 he resigned as Bailiff and stopped going to council meetings. Cited for debts in 1577, he started to sell off properties in 1578. The Elizabethans suffered a mysterious inflation in the 1570's; but there was another stress on John Shakespeare which lead to his fall in fortune.

In 1592 he was openly accused of recusancy. His excuse for not attending Church was he would meet his creditors there. But in April, 1757, workmen found a six-page booklet between the rafters and tiling of one of his houses in Henley Street. It was a Catholic profession of faith, signed with a mark by John Shakespeare. Denounced by many nineteenth century scholars as a forgery, (they needed their Shakespeare firmly Protestant) a Spanish version of 1661 (found in 1923) and another English one of 1638 (found in 1966) made people think again.* The Testament begins with a ringing affirmation of all the 'Papist trash' that Elizabeth and Burghley were eager to destroy:

'In the name of God, the Father, Son and Holy Ghost, the most holy and blessed Virgin Mary, Mother of God, the holy host of archangels, angels, patriarchs, prophets, evangelists, apostles and saints, martyrs and all the celestial court and company of heaven, I, John Shakespeare, an unworthy member of the Holy Catholic religion, do of my own accord, freely make this spiritual testament'.

John Shakespeare even names the Blessed Virgin and St. Winifred as executrixes of his will and promises to endure 'pain and agony like to a sharp, cutting razor' rather than renounce the Old Faith.

This testament originated with St. Carlo Borromeo in Milan. Campion brought it to England with him on his mission of 1580. He stayed with the Park Hall Ardens and with Sir William Catesby at Lapworth Hall, twelve miles north of Stratford-upon-Avon, so John Shakespeare most likely received his 'Challenge' from the hands of Campion himself. The pressure on the

---

* Eric Sams has found verbal parallels between the Spiritual Testament and the language of the Ghost in 'Hamlet'. *The Real Shakespeare* (1995).

Shakespeare family was the same pressure that was to destroy the life of the 2nd Earl of Southampton: the papal Bull of 1570.

We have only anecdotal evidence as to how this all affected young Will. But a picture does emerge.

●

Thomas Plume (1630-74), the Archdeacon of Rochester, in a notebook compiled around 1655-75, describes how Sir John Mennes met Shakespeare's father in his shop in Stratford-upon-Avon:

'He was a glover's son. Sir John Mennes saw once his old Father in his shop - a merry-cheeked old man - that said: Will was a good honest fellow, but he durst have crackt a jeast with him at any time.'

The first problem with the story is that Sir John Mennes was born 1st March, 1599 and John Shakespeare died in September, 1601. Plume probably meant Sir Matthew Mennes, his brother, born in 1593. But the second problem is that Plume wrote in what the Librarian at the Thomas Plume Library in Maldon calls an 'atrocious' shorthand: 'durst' could well be 'durnst'. But, either way, the use of the verb 'to dare' in describing the relationship suggests there was some distance between father and son.

It was different with Shakespeare's mother, Mary Arden. She had been the loved baby of her family. Her mother and father were both on second marriages when she was born. Her father had seven or eight daughters and her mother two sons and two daughters. But Mary was the only child of their union. Her father made her an executor of his will, though she was only in her twenties, and left her most of his property. She would have had all the confidence of an adored child. Having lost two daughters before William was born, Mary most likely passed on that adoration to her son at his birth in April, 1564. Smothered with feminine love, from his mother and his many aunts, Shakespeare was later to marry a woman nearly a decade older than himself.

Suggestion, though, of a tension in the young Shakespeare's life is provided by the Archdeacon of Coventry, Richard Davies (1688-1708). He claims, in a manuscript note left to Corpus Christi College in Oxford, Shakespeare was 'much given to unluckiness in stealing venison and rabbits particularly from Sir [Blank] Lucy who had him oft whipped and sometimes imprisoned and at last made him fly his native country to his great advancement'.

John Aubrey (1626-1697), the antiquarian, states in his 'Brief Lives' (1681) that Shakespeare's 'father was a butcher* and I have been told heretofore by some of the neighbours that when he was a boy he exercised his father's trade, but when he killed a calf he would do it in a high style and make a speech'. But Shakespeare later shows tremendous compassion for animals. In 'Venus and Adonis', Venus pleads with her reluctant lover to hunt the hare rather than the boar. Then, arguing against herself in her compassion, she feels the hare's terror as he -

> Stands on his hinder legs with list'ning ear,
> To hearken if his foes pursue him still.
> Anon their loud alarums he doth hear;
>> And now his grief may be compared well
>> To one sore sick, that hears the passing bell.
>> (ll. 698-702)

In 'As You Like It', Duke Senior is uneasy about hunting 'a poor sequester'd stag' even for food, and the First Lord's description of 'the hairy fool' weeping into 'the swift brook/Augmenting it with tears' (Act 2, Scene 1) is one of the most haunting passages Shakespeare ever wrote. Even in 'Love's Labour's Lost', the Princess of France shows guilt and remorse when she goes to shoot the rounded-up deer.

Perhaps the young Shakespeare made 'a speech' when he killed animals to close his heart to a repugnant act – in the way

---

* Malone suggests that when John Shakespeare's fortunes started to fall, he took to butchery as well as gloving.

butchers' boys in our times used to whistle on their blood-stained bikes.

Nicholas Rowe (1674-1718), the poet and dramatist, recounts in his 'Life' (1709) how John Shakespeare 'had bred' William "'tis true for some time at a free school where 'tis probable he acquired that little Latin he was master of...But the narrowness of his circumstances and the want of his assistance at home forced his father to withdraw him from hence, and unhappily prevented his further proficiency in that language'.

Shakespeare might have indulged in juvenile poaching because, like so many people who enter the theatre, he was frustrated at home.* But Catholic priests and schoolmasters have always been on the look-out for promising young men to save. And recruit...

●

Walter Roche and Simon Hunt were both Stratford school-masters from 1569-71 and 1571-5 respectively. Both were also Catholics and natives of Lancashire, a notoriously recusant county. Sir Ralph Saddler complained to Burghley in 1569 that in the whole county of Lancashire there were not even 'ten gentlemen, that do favour and allow of Her Majesty's proceedings in the cause of religion'. He added that 'the common people be ignorant, full of superstition, and altogether blinded by the old Popish doctrine'.

Simon Hunt left Stratford to train, with many other English noviciates, at the new Catholic seminary at Douai in Belgium, set up by Dr. William Allen in 1568 and financed by the Hoghtons of Lancashire with the wealth from their alum mines. When Shakespeare was fifteen, John Cottom, a Catholic from Dilworth and immediate neighbour to the Hoghtons, came to

---

* The poaching could also have been a Catholic revenge on Sir Thomas Lucy who was later to become an anti-Papist agent for Elizabeth after her 1591 Progress.

teach at the Stratford Grammar School. Cottom, whose Jesuit brother Thomas was to die for the Old Faith, saw a potential in this eccentric delinquent. The same year Shakespeare's eight year old sister Ann died.

Perhaps to save young Will from a grieving household, perhaps from Sir Thomas Lucy, perhaps even from the 'merry-cheeked old man' himself (whose ale-tasting duties might have got the better of him), Cottom recommended him as a likely Catholic lad to his Lancashire neighbours. There is a mention in Alexander de Hoghton's will of 1581 of a 'William Shakeshafte', along with musical instruments and 'all manner of playe clothes' which he leaves to his half-brother Thomas. If Thomas does not want them, then Sir Thomas Hesketh of Rufford 'shall have the same instruments and playe clothes. And I most heartily require the said Sir Thomas to be friendly unto ffoke Gwyllome and William Shakeshafte now dwelling with me and either to take them into his service or else to help them to some good master as my trust is he will'. The Hoghton family tradition is that 'Shakeshafte' was Shakespeare. William's grand-father, Richard, used the same form of surname – and the mention of play clothes and musical instruments in the same breath as 'Shakeshafte' is unlikely to be simple coincidence. As an actor Shakespeare would have played women's rôles – boys' voices did not break till much later in Tudor times – and this could have given him an understanding of women that he was later to explore in his own plays. But, at fifteen, part of his job might have been to entertain the children. History was not taught at school: Shakespeare could have used the 'play clothes' to teach the children the story of their family. He might even have amused the children of Ferdinando, Lord Strange, a neigh-bour of the Hoghtons and the Patron whose acting company first performed a play of his in London.

Campion stayed at Hoghton Hall in 1581. Shakespeare would have witnessed at first hand the desperate beauty of his chivalric pledge to Elizabeth that young Englishmen were prepared to die a martyr's death to ensure her conversion to Rome:

'Many innocent hands are lifted up to heaven for you daily by those English students, whose posterity shall never die, which beyond seas, gathering virtue and sufficient knowledge for the purpose, are determined never to give you over, but either to win you, or to die upon your pikes.'

Later that year Campion himself died upon her pikes, hanged drawn and quartered. Two years later Edward Arden – the man who links Shakespeare's family with the Southamptons – was also executed for his faith. Like Lord Montague, he had kept a secret Catholic priest, Hugh Hall, this time disguised as a gardener. Tremendous pressure must have been put on the young Shakespeare to become one of Campion's missionary priests: but, sympathetic as he was to the Old Faith, the martyr's crown was not for him. Fulke Gillam, it seems, not Shakespeare, got the job with Hesketh. Shakespeare was back in Stratford and obliged to marry Anne Hathaway by December, 1582. Their daughter Susanna was baptised on 26th May, 1583. In Shakespeare's absence, his parents had made up for the loss of his sister Ann by producing a baby boy, Edmund, no doubt named after Campion. No longer his mother's 'special' son, Shakespeare had turned to Anne Hathaway, an old family friend.

It is unlikely Shakespeare would have worked for his father again: given the decline in the gloving business, this would have been counter-productive. Significantly, none of John Shakespeare's sons took up his father's trade. (Gilbert became a haberdasher and Edmund an actor). Malone believes that Shakespeare, because of the extensive knowledge of the law revealed in his writing, worked as a lawyer's clerk at Stratford-upon-Avon. But when the twins Hamnet and Judith, named after two recusant family friends, came along in 1585, Shakespeare needed to find a better paid job.

Anecdotal evidence has him running away to London to join the theatre. But the source is the flamboyant, Oxford-born, Poet Laureate, playwright, theatre manager, contraband-runner, tavern-brawler and terminal syphilitic, Sir William Davenant (1606-1668) who, as well as claiming to possess a fan letter from King James VI and I to Shakespeare, styled himself the playwright's bastard son. He would, according to Aubrey, even go so far as to say when 'pleasant over a glass of wine with his most intimate friends…that he writ with the very spirit of Shakespeare'. It is significant that neither Aubrey himself, who knew Davenant, nor Rowe, who questioned his protégé, the actor Betterton, used Davenant's most famous story – that Shakespeare held the horses for rich play-goers at the door of the Playhouse – in either of their 'Lives'.

It is much more likely that Shakespeare exploited the complex network of recusancy. He had a good reference from the Hoghtons, he was 'related' to Mary Southampton and his father was an ardent Catholic. The Montagues and Southamptons had plotted with the Northern Lords to place Mary, Queen of Scots on the throne. Lady Stanley had been Mary Southampton's grandmother and Lady Lucy Neville and Thomas Stanley her great grandparents. Campion was also a common factor. He had met with the Ardens, the Southamptons, the Hoghtons and the Shakespeares. Shakespeare's other sad link with the Southamptons was the martyrdom, two years earlier, of their 'shared' relative, Edward Arden. Shakespeare probably contacted the Hoghtons and they contacted Mary Southampton.

But what sort of job was there for a twenty-one year old in Titchfield?

# CHAPTER 5.

# SAINTS AND SINNERS

Titchfield needed a schoolmaster. In 1542, eight years before he went mad, John Leland described how his old University friend, the 1st Earl of Southampton, had built 'on the exact site of the former Premonstratensian Abbey of Titchfield....a very grand house, with battlements and a goodly door....There is a Grammar School close to the riverbank and there is a park, although its soil is rather poor and heathy'. John Leland was also the friend of Hampshire-born Nicholas Udall (1506-1556). Udall and Leland, later famous for writing Christmas pastimes and interludes, had provided an entertainment for the Coronation of Anne Boleyn. Udall wanted to be a monk: but in 1534 he got a job as a schoolmaster at Eton and then things started to go wrong. He failed to pay debts, appeared before a judge and was 'outlawed' in the City of London. It was his relationship with his scholars, though, that was to cause most problems. One of them, Tom Tusser, in his '500 Points', describes how:

> From Paul's I was to Eton sent
> To learn straight ways, the Latin phrase,
> When fifty-three stripes given to me
>    At once I had:
> For fault but small, or none at all,
> It came to pass, thus beat I was,
> See Udall see, the mercies of thee,
>    To me poor lad.

It was not a taste for flagellation, though, that led to Udall's downfall. In March, 1541 two 'old boys' from Eton, John Hoord and Thomas Cheney, together with Udall's servant, stole silver images and other plate from the college and sold them to a London goldsmith. The three confessed to the theft: Udall himself became 'suspect to be a counsel of the robbery'. He was cleared of this crime, but confessed 'he did commit buggery with the said Cheney sundry times heretofore and of late the 6th day of this present month in this present year at London: whereupon he was committed to the Marshalsea.' This document in the Public Record Office, Kew, has 'the felony of' crossed out before 'buggery'. The authorities took a lenient view and Udall was soon out of prison. His next post was at the Titchfield Grammar School.

There is a four page folio letter (1543) from Udall to Sir Thomas Wriothesley headed 'Right Worshipful and my Singular Good Master'. Udall thanks Wriothesley for trying, unsuccessfully, 'for my restitution to the Room of Schoolmaster at Eton'. He admits he has deserved Wriothesley's 'displeasure and indignation', but adds:

'Since the....intercession of my good friends...to my knowledge I have not eftsons [since] offended. And in what heaviness, in what sorrow, in what pensiveness of heart I have lived since my coming from Titchfield were I able to express (as in deed no man is) it would be to your mastership incredible'.

Leland was certainly one of the 'good friends' who interceded for Udall. Another of them could even have been the schoolboy Thomas Cheney (Jane Southampton's maiden name was 'Cheney' and Udall's pupils, despite his failings, adored him). The Wriothesley/Southamptons, taking over the Grammar School from the monks at the Dissolution of the Abbey, had to maintain it themselves.* They employed Nicholas Udall and it

---

* We know that the 3rd Earl of Southampton helped with the maintenance of a Grammar School in Newport on the Isle of Wight in 1619. *Shakespeare and the Earl of Southampton* G.P.V. Akrigg (1968)

was probably at Titchfield Grammar School that he lapsed into his old 'excesses and abuses'. He was back in London by 1545.

Udall wrote 'Ralph Roister Doister', one of the first English language comedies, based on the Latin authors Terence and Plautus. Because of its 'decent and moralising tone' Scheurweghs, the Udall scholar, is convinced the play was written for schoolboys: but he does not know where it was first performed. It cannot have been Eton as plays there were performed in Latin until 1560. Scheurweghs dates the play after 1541 but doubts it can be as late as 1551 (when Udall became Prebend of Windsor). He is convinced that it was written as a Christmas entertainment: but concludes that 'it is impossible to connect it with a particular school'. If he had known about the Titchfield Grammar School, the 1st Earl's amateur acting and Jane's enjoyment of Christmas masques, he might have thought differently. It could well have been a drunken Christmas production of 'Ralph Roister Doister' with the Titchfield schoolboys that led to Udall's downfall.

He ended up as Headmaster of Westminster School.

●

The next Titchfield schoolmaster, Hierom Colas, a Frenchman, caused political scandals instead. The 1st Earl's death on 30th July, 1550, three years into the Protestant reign of Edward VI, was followed by a Privy Council order to local spies to arrest Colas and 'assure' him 'that the whole thing is revealed to the Lords'.

'The whole thing' was most likely a plot to put the infant Mary, Queen of Scots on the throne. Jane Southampton, in a letter to the Privy Council's William Petrie, pleaded ignorance of the whole Colas affair. But this was most likely a bluff. Afterwards, when Mary Tudor came to the throne, Jane could openly employ a Catholic schoolmaster and a household of Catholic servants, loyal to her and the Old Faith. But on Elizabeth's Accession in 1558, everything reverted to secrecy. In the fallout Jane rescued the distinguished Catholic Divine Dr. Alban Langdale and gave him a job as her family Chaplain. Langdale, who had disputed with Ridley and Cranmer, was reduced to celebrating furtive masses in the tiny 'Place House' chapel. In his sermons he would have re-iterated his belief, published in his pamphlets, that only priests, not laymen, should be martyrs to the Faith.

Swithin Wells, whom Jane's son, the 2nd Earl, appointed as tutor a few years later, had fatally different views. Born around 1536, the sixth son of Thomas Wells of Bambridge near Winchester, Swithin came from a staunch Catholic family, long-term recusants and close friends of the Southamptons. The Earl later made Gilbert, Swithin's brother, one of the executors to his will. Bishop Richard Challoner (1691-1781), quoting Thomas Stanney, wrote in his 'Memoirs of Missionary Priests' (1741) that Swithin Wells was educated from 'infancy' in 'the liberal sciences'. He then travelled to Italy, partly to visit the shrines and partly 'to learn the language'. He was 'a witty man skilled in diverse languages' who 'gave a good example to the gentry'. On his return from Italy 'he was employed in the service of several persons of quality and after some time for his skill in language and for his eloquence he was desired by the most noble Earl of Southampton, a most constant professor of the Catholic faith, to live in his house, as he did, much to his own commendation for several years'.

Wells had sufficient self-control to abandon his love of hawking and hunting to indoctrinate young men into Catholicism. His school was more like a training ground for suicide missionaries, one of whose graduates 'gained the crown of martyrdom'. After his marriage, Wells taught 'young gentlemen the belles-lettres and music' and used his own house as a meeting place for priests: two or three Masses were celebrated there each day. He became so well known as a Catholic activist that it was dangerous for clerics, in disguise, to travel with him. He was certainly with the Southampton family during the Mary, Queen of Scots plot. In 1576, two years after the death of the Dowager Countess Jane and when Harry Southampton was three, he moved to Monkton Farleigh, near Bath, where he kept his own school.

The 2nd Earl's death, five years later, produced a chilling note from a meeting of the Privy Council. They ordered the Recorder to raid the Southamptons' London home, apprehend anyone who was practising against the State and to search for 'books, letters and ornaments for massing'.

The Earl had dictated a mysterious clause in his will 'that William my beggar's boy be kept found and brought up by my executors at school until he shall come to the age of twenty and one years and then I will and bequeath him 40 marks of lawful money of England to be paid at the same age if he shall so long live.'

Why should the Earl educate a beggar boy until his majority and then give him the equivalent of £20,000?

Wells, I believe, was working for Rome at Titchfield Grammar School. He would recruit his brightest pupils and send them down the River Meon to be ordained as priests at Douai and then return, as missionaries, to certain death in England. William was intended to be one of them.

The year after the Earl's death the Privy Council ordered the Sheriff of Wiltshire to search 'for one Wells a Schoolmaster and dangerous Papist' and to raid his school at Monkton Farleigh.

Wells either escaped – or convinced the authorities of his innocence. On the 9th August, 1586 he was being 'examined' in London. He stated that, on giving up his school at Monkton Farleigh, he had, since 1582, 'lived amongst his friends, and now liveth upon the benevolence of his friends, as of his brother Gilbert Wells and other of his friends'. On 14th August suspected recusants were questioned about 'their knowledge of Swithin Wells and others who were entertained in his mistress's [Mary Southampton's London] house'. Mary Southampton had clearly been one of the 'friends' who had helped Swithin Wells. Now his 'mistress' was under suspicion herself. She had given him back his old job as Titchfield schoolmaster. That was part of her 'benevolence'.

In 1587 the Privy Council notes record the 'Confession of Swithin Wells, a recusant, concerning the places of abode and his dealings with the recusants'. He had been tortured, the heat was on the Southampton family, and the Titchfield schoolboys badly needed a schoolmaster.

# CHAPTER 6.

# THE PLACE WHERE

John Aubrey, after talking to the actor William Beeston, (whose father Christopher had played with the Lord Chamberlain's Men in 1598) wrote that Shakespeare 'had been in his younger years a Schoolmaster in the country'.

Shakespeare's twins were born around the time Swithin Wells started to get into serious trouble with the Privy Council. I believe Mary Southampton gave Shakespeare Wells's old teaching job in Titchfield. She was clearly a forceful, passionate woman, with a deep feeling for language, whose husband's family had always delighted in plays. A masque had been performed at her own London wedding to the 2nd Earl when everyone, including mounted knights, wore white. Shakespeare, with what Henry Chettle (c.1560-c.1607), the printer and playwright, describes in 'A Kind Hart's Dream' (1592) as a 'demeanour' that was 'civil' and an 'uprightness in dealing which argues his honesty and his facetious grace in writing' would have appealed to Mary, as he did to 'divers of worship.'

And Shakespeare would have been taken with her - beautiful, and about the same age as his own wife. In his plays he returns time and again to the theme of the chaste woman accused, like Mary, of adultery. His high-spirited comedy heroines, taking on a man's world and twisting it about, could well have been inspired by the Countess.

Shakespeare, as schoolmaster, was taking over an established position. At Titchfield you not only taught the boys of the town; you had to entertain the Southamptons as well. As a poor relation, Shakespeare would have been under a double pressure. Like Benedick in 'Much Ado About Nothing' and even Rosalind

in 'As You Like It', he would have felt obliged to be witty as well
as to fetch and carry. Robert Greene (c.1558-1592), in his
famous death-bed 'upstart crow' attack,* describes Shakespeare
as 'an absolute Johannes fac totum' – and Shakespeare himself is
always massively sympathetic to jesters forced to entertain their
'betters'. In 'Twelfth Night' Viola says of the clown Feste:

> This fellow is wise enough to play the fool,
> And to do that well, craves a kind of wit:
> He must observe their mood on whom he jests,
> The quality of persons, and the time,
> And like the haggard, [hawk] check at every feather
> That comes before his eye. This is a practice
> As full of labour as a wise man's art...
>
> (Act 3, Scene 1)

Shakespeare, like Feste in Olivia's household, had to entertain a family recovering from the loss of it's male head, run by a
courageous young woman and threatened by the kill-joy
Protestantism/Puritanism of Burghley/Malvolio.

There is also stunning evidence that Shakespeare, perhaps
utilising his Stratford-upon-Avon lawyer clerk experience, acted
as secretary for the family as well. On 27th June, 1592, Harry
Southampton wrote to one of Burghley's agents to ask for
money for the upkeep of his crumbling Beaulieu estate. He
dictated the letter, and signed it in flashy, fashionable italics. But
the body of the letter, as Eric Sams, discovered in 1981, is in
exactly in the same hand as Shakespeare's will and signature.
Shakespeare signed the document 'By me': so unless the same
clerk was in London in 1592 working for Southampton and at
Shakespeare's death-bed in Warwickshire twenty-four years

---

* '...for there is an upstart Crow, beautified with our feathers, that with his tiger's heart
wrapped in a Player's hide, supposes he is well able to bombast out a blank verse as the best
of you: and being an absolute Johannes fac totum, is in his own conceit the only Shake-scene
in a country.' Robert Greene *Greene's Groatsworth of Wit*, (20th September, 1592).

later, busily forging his client's signature, the conclusion must be that Shakespeare drafted Southampton's letter.*

Mary Southampton, knowing about Shakespeare's service at Hoghton Hall, and sensing his ability with words, encouraged him to write plays for the local schoolboys about Titchfield and her family. (The 1737 groundplan of 'Place House' even includes an upstairs 'Playhouse Room'). She would have given Shakespeare access to the family's books which included her mother-in-law Jane's copy of Chaucer. 'Troilus and Cressida' was based on 'Troilus and Criseyde' and 'The Two Noble Kinsmen', which Shakespeare wrote with John Fletcher, on 'The Knight's Tale' in 'The Canterbury Tales'. Chaucer's translation of the French medieval love-poem, 'The Romance of the Rose', has also clearly influenced 'Love's Labour's Lost'. In the poem the 'Lover', in a highly eroticised landscape, makes his way into a garden to pluck a rose, a symbol of his mistress's vagina. When Dumaine, one of the young Lords, writes a poem to Katharine he compares his love to a breeze that penetrates the leaves of a rose – and wishes he too could enter the secret parts of the flower:

> But alack! My hand is sworn
> Ne'er to pluck thee from thy thorn

Mary Southampton herself probably suggested a subject for one of Shakespeare's earliest plays - Henry VI, the saintly monarch who had been married at Titchfield Abbey a hundred and fifty years earlier. Six of Mary's ancestors feature in the 'Henry VI' trilogy: the Earl of Salisbury, Sir John Stanley,

---

* 'The handwriting in the body of the letter appears to me to be that of William Shakespeare. The 'feel' or general appearance of the writing, which includes the size of the script, slant, space between lines and words, configuration of letters, stroke pattern, speed of the writing, is the same as in Shakespeare's will'. Affidavit (30th June, 1986) of Charles Hamilton, New York documents expert, quoted by Eric Sams. The letter is in the British Library – Volume 71, Lansdowne Manuscripts. It has a '72' marked in the top right corner.

Marquis of Montague, Lord Hastings, Sir William Stanley and Lady Grey.

●

Harry Southampton was fifteen when he was granted his Master's Degree from Cambridge in June, 1589. He joined the Inns of Court, a gentlemen's club rather than a place for serious study and, no longer imprisoned at Burghley's house in the summer breaks, he could visit his own estates. On 14th October, 1590, Mary Southampton wrote to Burghley on her son's departure to London, thanking him for 'the long time' he 'had intrusted' her son to her. Harry had clearly rushed straight to Titchfield the moment he graduated. It was there and then, I believe, he first met 'cousin Will'. And when Shakespeare, in the words of Sonnet 104, first 'eyed' the young man's 'eye.'

Mary's letter to Burghley is dated 14th October: Harry's 17th Birthday was 6th October. Lord Montague had written earlier to Burghley on 16th September, thanking him for having granted his grandson a year from 'last winter' to consider marriage to Elizabeth de Vere 'in respect of his young years'. As Montague observes, that year is nearly up. Shakespeare, commissioned by Mary Southampton and her father, wrote seventeen sonnets as a parting 'present' on Harry's crucial 17th Birthday. He employed the sonnet form because Southampton's boyhood hero, the soldier-poet Sir Philip Sidney (1554-1586) had used it in his cycle 'Astrophil and Stella'. No doubt young Harry was flattered by Shakespeare's continual reference to his beauty: but the argument of the poems, urging the boy to marry, would have met with the young Lord's displeasure, perhaps fury.

In the first line of the first sonnet Shakespeare writes: 'From fairest creatures we desire increase'. The 'we' would certainly include Mary Southampton and Montague. It might also have suggested the hated Burghley and the royal 'we' of the Queen herself. Shakespeare was siding with Harry's family and the Protestant establishment. But his habit in his plays is finally to empathise with the victims he initially attacks. I believe this is what happened with Southampton.

This empathy was to change Shakespeare's life.

●

The following year Shakespeare invented 'The Siege of Rouen' in 'Henry VI Part One'. No such siege had ever taken place in Henry VI's time: but one was taking place in 1591, and Essex, Southampton's beloved friend, was fighting there. As Southampton had been forbidden to fight in France, Shakespeare brought the war to him. The schoolboys and young friends of the Earl re-enacted the siege, with trumpets, horses and swordplay, by scaling the fortified walls of 'Place House'. The deaths of Talbot, the diminutive hero of 'Henry VI' who sacks Rouen, and his brave son who refuses to abandon his father, were Shakespeare's warning to Southampton about the deadly consequences of chivalry in the age of the bullet and the canon. The English, armed only with swords, are surrounded by French artillery. Talbot compares their plight to deer rounded up for certain slaughter on one of Elizabeth's 'hunts':

> How are we park'd and bounded in a pale –
> A little herd of England's timorous deer,
> Maz'd with a yelping kennel of French curs!
>
> (Act 4, Scene 2)

This was an oblique criticism of Sidney who, much to Elizabeth's disdain, had actually died of chivalry five years earlier at Zutphen at the age of 32. He had noticed that an older soldier had no leg armour so, in an act of comradely bravura, tore off his own. He was immediately shot in the leg and later died of the wound. He was said by his friend, Sir Fulke Greville, to have given his share of water to another injured soldier, saying 'Thy necessity is greater than mine'.

The language of the Talbot section of the play is deliberately written in a declamatory style, and the characterisation ('goodies and baddies') is kept simple because Shakespeare knew schoolboys would act it.* The play is written from the aristocrats' point of view, not from the ordinary people, because Shakespeare naturally identifies with the interests of his new family. Mary Southampton most likely encouraged Shakespeare to develop the piece for adult actors. She also probably pulled strings, as only she knew how, to get her cousin, Lord Strange, to stage the play at the Rose in March, 1592. Even the genius of Shakespeare is proof of the old theatrical adage 'it's not what you know but who you know'. Or even more important, to whom you are 'related'.

●

In January, 1592 Essex returned from the Siege of Rouen. Gervase Markham (c.1568-1637) – a soldier turned writer who also enjoyed Southampton's patronage – claims in 'Honour in his Perfection' (1624) that Essex had 'brought Rouen to that low ebb of safety that he offered to give it to the King when he pleased.' The King of Navarre, according to Markham, declined the Earl's invitation on the chivalric grounds that he 'wanted to win France, not to conquer France'. Giovanni Mocenigo, the Venetian Ambassador to France, writing to the Doge in 1592, tells us what really happened:

'The English were the first to scale the walls and at the point of the sword they penetrated the guardhouse of the enemy...The following night the position was re-captured, in spite of the

---

* Jane Howell, in her masterly television production of the play in the 1970's, directed this section of the work as a playground romp.

courage shown by the English, who did all that became brave and experienced soldiers. This misfortune was attributed to the faulty construction of the defences, which, being made of barrels, were easily fired and burned...The Earl of Essex and the English [were] in great distress for their honour's sake'.

Essex was brave, but not bright. The King of Navarre ordered Armand de Gontaut, maréchal de Biron, to seize the position instead. Also fighting at the siege were Henri d'Orlèans, duc de Longueville and Charles, duc de Mayenne.

Navarre, Biron, Longueville and de Mayenne. Readers familiar with 'Love's Labour's Lost' will recognise, buried here, the names of the four young Lords in the play - Navarre, Berowne, Longaville and Dumaine.

For those less familiar, a synopsis of the play follows.

●

*The young King of Navarre and his three Lords, (Berowne, Dumaine and Longaville) have taken an oath to withdraw from the world and women to study for three years. Berowne has his doubts, but goes along with the scheme. He reminds the King that the Princess of France and her Ladies are due on a diplomatic mission. Dull, the slow-witted Constable, arrives with a letter from their boastful Spanish guest, Don Armado, who has discovered Costard the swain making love to Jaquenetta, a country girl, in the King's own Park. The King sentences Costard to a week's fasting and custody.*

*Don Armado admits to his quick-witted pageboy, Moth, that he is in love with Jaquenetta. Dull arrives with Costard and the girl. The King has ordered Don Armado to supervise Costard's imprisonment while Dull will keep Jaquenetta at the Lodge. Don Armado makes heavy-handed overtures to Jaquenetta – but she rebuffs him.*

*The beautiful Princess of France arrives with her Ladies, Rosaline, Katharine and Maria and her effeminate factotum, Boyet. The King explains to the Princess that, because of his vow, he can only entertain her outside the doors of his court. She demands the return of Aquitaine from the King: her bed-ridden father, she claims, has paid for the land – proof of which will arrive the following day. The smitten Lords seek information about the Ladies from Boyet, who announces to the Princess that the King of Navarre has fallen in love with her. Don Armado sets Costard free to carry his love-letter to Jaquenetta: Berowne then gives the swain a love sonnet to take to Rosaline. In a soliloquy Berowne confesses his guilty, reluctant love for the wayward, dark-skinned beauty.*

*The next day the Princess and her ladies shoot deer. Costard arrives with what he thinks is Berowne's letter to Rosaline: but he has mixed it up with Don Armado's letter to Jaquenetta. Armado's extravagant professions of love provide much sport for the Ladies. The pedantic schoolmaster, Holofernes, has been watching the deer hunt with Sir Nathaniel, a time-serving Curate. Dull insists that the deer shot was a pricket (a two year old red-deer) and the schoolmaster composes an extempore verse on its death. Jaquenetta arrives with Costard, and asks the curate to read Don Armado's letter to her – in reality Berowne's love-sonnet to Rosaline. Holofernes orders Jaquenetta to take Berowne's 'treasonable' poem to the King.*

*Berowne, agonised by his perjury, is composing another sonnet to Rosaline in the Park when he sees the King and hides in a tree. The King reads his poem to the Princess, but sees Longaville and hides. Longaville reads his poem to Maria, but sees Dumaine and also hides. Dumaine reads his poem to Katharine, Longaville emerges to denounce him, the King denounces Longaville then Berowne, dropping from his tree, denounces all three. Jaquenetta and Costard arrive with Berowne's sonnet to Rosaline – and Berowne has to confess he is as guilty as everyone else. The Lords argue as to whose mistress is the most beautiful: but then ask Berowne to justify their perjury. In a beautiful passage, Berowne praises the transfiguring power of love. The Lords resolve to woo the Ladies.*

*Holofernes, Sir Nathaniel and Dull return from the lunch they have enjoyed with the father of a pupil. Don Armado, accompanied by Moth and Costard, tells the schoolteacher that the King has asked him to provide an entertainment for the Princess. Holofernes suggests the Masque of the Nine Worthies.*

*The Princess and her companions mockingly compare the favours – and verses – they have received from their lovers. Boyet arrives, massively excited: he has learnt the Lords intend to fool the Ladies by dressing as Russians and wooing them in disguise. The Princess plans to outwit the Lords. All the ladies will mask and exchange favours: that way the men will woo the wrong women. She also orders her women to turn their backs on the Lords and refuse to dance with them.*

*A trumpet sounds – and Blackamoors enter 'with music', followed by the 'Russians'. The women carry out their plan and the men depart in an embarrassed fury. The women, returning the favours to the original owners, retire to their tents. The King and the Lords return out of disguise. The King asks Boyet for an audience with the Princess – and while he is gone, Berowne attacks the factotum's sycophancy.*

*The Princess and her Ladies reveal they knew that the Russians were the Lords in disguise. The men are further humiliated when they discover that each has courted the wrong lady. A potential fight between Berowne and Boyet is prevented by the performance of the Masque. To the brutal mocking of the Lords, Costard plays Pompey the Great, Sir Nathaniel, Alexander the Great, Moth, the infant Hercules, Holofernes, Judas Maccabaeus and Armado, Hector. Costard suddenly announces that Jaquenetta is two months pregnant – and names Armado as the father. The Lords urge Armado to challenge him – and Costard strips down to his shirt. Armado admits he cannot 'uncase' like Costard: he is too poor to wear a shirt under his doublet.*

*Marcade arrives with the news of the death of the Princess's father, and the mood of the play darkens. The Lords want to pursue their love-suits: but the women impose tasks on them in the coming year to prove their love. The Lords agree; but Berowne thinks a year is 'too long for a play'.*

*'Love's Labour's Lost' ends with the beautiful songs of Spring and Winter, composed by Holofernes and Sir Nathaniel.*

●

Why did Shakespeare name the four young Lords in his play after the four French Generals who fought at the Siege of Rouen?

It is my belief that Southampton, encouraged by his mother, invited his friend Essex down to Titchfield to celebrate his 'great work' in France as part of what Markham calls 'the admiration and applause of both kingdoms.' Shakespeare wrote 'Love's Labour's Lost' in honour of the event. By naming all the Generals who had taken part in the Siege of Rouen, Shakespeare is acknowledging the military 'triumph' of the Guest of Honour.

He also celebrates Essex's Commander, the King of Navarre, by mentioning Hercules five times in the play – and casting Moth as the infant God in the Masque of the Nine Worthies★. As well as being 'Surnamed the Great', the King of Navarre styled himself, as we can see from contemporary illustrations, as 'Herculi Gallico' - the Gallic Hercules.

Two other details link Navarre in the play with the historical King. The Princess asks:

> Was that the King who spurred his horse so hard

---

★ Hercules was never considered a Worthy. The official list includes Joshua, David and Judas Maccabaeus; Hector, Alexander and Julius Caesar; Arthur, Charlemagne and Godfrey of Bouillon. As John Dryden put it, 'Nine worthies were they called of different rites /Three Jews, three Pagans and three Christian knights'. *The Flower and the Leaf: Fables Ancient and Modern* (1674)

Against the steep-uprising of the hill?

Henri was famous for riding his horses 'hard'. And the letter the King sends to the Princess containing -

> as much love in rhyme
> As would be crammed up in a sheet of paper
> Writ both sides, the leaf, margent and all

- refers to Navarre's habit of covering every inch of his letters with close-scrawled script.

But why is 'Biron' strangely anglicised to 'Berowne?' And how should it be pronounced? Most productions take the simple way out. The King says:

> My love, her mistress, is a gracious moon
> She an attending star scarce seen a light

Berowne replies:

> My eyes are then no eyes, nor I Berowne
> O but for my love day would turn to night

'Berowne' is made to rhyme with 'moon'. But Shakespeare was often cavalier in his rhyming. Rosaline says:

> Another of these students at that time
> Was there with him if I have heard a truth
> Berowne they call him, but a merrier man,
> Within the limits of becoming mirth
> I never spent an hour's talk withal

'Berowne' here should be pronounced 'Brown', suggesting someone sombre or sad. This is reinforced by Berowne's address to Rosaline after news has arrived of the King's death: 'Studies, my lady? Mistress, look on me'. Berowne is implying Rosaline is in a 'brown study'. Or should that be a 'Browne study'? The Elizabethans and Jacobeans loved all sorts of word play. Even when the 3rd Earl died, carrying home the body of his son from

Holland, the author of their panegyric could not resist turning their two names into an anagram:

Henrye James Wriothesley = 'Here I see many Worthies Ly'

Shakespeare, in creating Berowne, is playing on the maiden name of Mary Southampton - BROWNE. Sir Henry Browne, her brother, was the link with the Ardens, and Elizabeth had knighted George Browne, Montague's second son, on her Progress to Cowdray the year before.

Berowne, in the play, argues that the King should mix with women rather than retire with his men. This is the argument of Shakespeare's first sonnets to Southampton, and the argument of Mary Browne/Southampton. Desperate about Burghley's fine and desperate the Southampton line would die out, she clearly commissioned the play to persuade her son to marry. Shakespeare was happy to oblige as his own livelihood was threatened as well. He gives a common English name to the one Lord who speaks 'common sense'. And declares his allegiance to one of the oldest Catholic families in the land.

●

The dating of 'Love's Labour's Lost' has always been a problem: the text we have is not the original one. The frontispiece to the First Quarto printing says:

*As it was presented before her Highness this last Christmas*
*Newly corrected and augmented*
*By W. Shakespeare*
*Imprinted at London by W.W.*
*For Cuthbert Burby 1598*

The script has been reworked for a Christmas performance at Court, probably Christmas of 1597. In Shakespeare's day, the New Year started on 25th March, Lady Day: so 'last Christmas' could be 1597 or 1598. Elizabeth's pleasures were intricately bound up with politics: by ordering a performance of the play she could check up both on Southampton and Shakespeare.

Scripts change to an astonishing degree in their working life. If there is a revival of a play, and the playwright is still alive, he will always want to 'improve' it and bring it 'up-to-date'.* Any line, or any incident, in 'Love's Labour's Lost' could have been changed days, or even hours, before the performance for the Queen, so we cannot date the play by the text alone. The Editor of the new Arden Edition puts the first performance in 1594, but admits that the evidence is 'relatively thin'. I want to suggest an earlier date: 1592. At that time Henri of Navarre was a popular English hero, a Protestant fighting Catholics. In July, 1593 Navarre astounded the English by converting to Catholicism with the reported justification that 'Paris is worth a Mass'. No Elizabethan author after the Papal Bull of 1570, especially one with Catholic connections, would dare use the name of a Catholic as the hero of his comedy. Elizabeth, at the Christmas revival, would know that she was watching an old play.

I want to suggest an exact date – and an exact circumstance - in 1592.

---

* Sir Terence Rattigan, for example, when I directed his great play 'The Browning Version' at The King's Head Theatre in Islington in 1976, wanted to turn it into a suburban 'Heda Gabler' by having Millie Crocker-Harris burn her husband's translation of 'The Agamemnon'. He was dissuaded.

# CHAPTER 7.

# THE TIME WHEN

When we read the play in Titchfield, one of the most striking features was the number of times fairs, and everything associated with them, were mentioned. Costard wants to buy a carnation ribbon. He gives Moth money to buy a gingerbread Saint. The Princess refers to the gifts from the Lords as 'fairings' (gifts from fairs). Moth also quotes the Morris cry: 'The hobbyhorse is forgot' and Holofernes the country dance 'Trip and go'. Berowne, in describing his mistress Rosaline, says all 'complexions/ Do meet as at a fair in her fair cheek'. In attacking Boyet he describes him as 'wit's pedlar' who 'retails his wares/At wakes and wassails, meetings, markets fairs'. Dull offers his tabor so the Worthies can 'Dance the hay'. Costard practises his bargaining tactics to buy an 'inkle' (linen tape).

In addition the word 'fair' itself, with all it's meanings, is used a staggering 67 times, more than in any other play by Shakespeare. 'Troilus and Cressida' comes second with 48 mentions of 'fair' and 'Romeo and Juliet' third with 43. 'Julius Caesar', bottom of the table, only has 2. It seemed obvious that the play was originally performed within the context of a fair. Had there been one at Titchfield?

I looked up old Fair Schedules in the London Library and British Library. The earliest mention I could find of a Titchfield Fair was 3rd May, 1709 in John Bridges 'A Book of Fairs'. By 1759, following the change in the Calendar in 1742 when England 'lost' eleven days, the Fair had changed to the 14th May and, according to 'Owen's Book of Fairs', stayed that way till at least 1860. It was a 'fixed' fair, held on the same date every year, not one that followed movable Church Festivals, and was exclusively for 'Toys'. Other fairs at Titchfield were for dealing in animals, or 'Mop Fairs', when servants, dressed in their Sunday best, lined up to be hired.

I then searched dozens of Elizabethan 'almanacks' with their typical Tudor jumble of Church calendars, astrological predictions and folk remedies. They contained the dates of fairs, but only the major ones. So I had no proof that a fair had existed in Shakespeare's time in Titchfield.

Then I stumbled on the evidence on the Internet. The people of Titchfield, for the first time in living memory, had revived an old fair on 10th July, 1999 in the grounds of Titchfield Abbey. Completely ignorant of this, my team had read 'Love's Labour's Lost' on that very spot a week later.

I checked the evidence at the Public Record Office at Kew. The Calendar of Charter Rolls for 1447 records a royal proclamation by King Henry VI, thanking the Abbot and the convent of Titchfield for 'much courtesy and diligence' shown to him and his wife during their marriage and honeymoon. To make the monks 'more bound to pray for the health of himself and his consort and for their souls after death', Henry grants a series of 'liberties and amenities'. They include 'one tun of red wine of Gascony' for the Abbot and the Abbey, the right to any flotsam and gettson washed up on the Titchfield shores and 'a yearly fair' on the Vigil and the Feast of Corpus Christi 'and the three days following.'

The wonderful thing about a fair, which could only be granted, or repealed, by the monarch, was that it enabled ordinary people to make money by selling their household bread, beer, wine and cakes. At any other time it was forbidden. Corpus Christi itself falls on the Thursday in the week after Whitsun week. Although it was a relatively new Festival, (Pope Urban 4th ordered the whole Church to celebrate Corpus

Christi in 1264), by Henry VI's time it was the most important event in the Church Year. The sacrament and religious statues, liberated from the confines of the Church, were processed around the streets and Mystery Plays performed by Guilds in the open air.* This was far too Papist for young Edward VI: he abolished Corpus Christi and replaced it with 'Whitsunday', officially named for the first time in his 1549 Prayer Book.

Whitsunday – originally White Sunday because everyone wore white to Church – is the reason 'white' is mentioned twelve times in the play, often in relation to white clothing. When Berowne sends a love message via Costard to Rosaline he says:

> And to her white hand see thou do commend
> This sealed up counsel

The actual poem is addressed to 'the snow-white hand of the most beauteous Lady Rosaline'. As Rosaline is dark-skinned, she must have been wearing white gloves.

A white glove was also a symbol of a fair. To this day, in a ceremony called 'the shaking of the glove', a huge white hand is waved from the Guildhall in Barnstaple to begin the September Chartered Fair. It was a sign to illiterate folk that buying and selling could begin.

The people of Titchfield simply transferred the Corpus Christi celebrations to Whitsun, in the same way as the people of Chester did with their Mystery Cycle. Granted only 150 years before the date of 'Love's Labour's Lost', the Corpus Fair would be jealously guarded, not least by the local Vicar who could make money from the sale of his own Church Ale.

For Shakespeare, Whitsun was also the time for play-acting. In 'The Winter's Tale' Perdita says:

---

* The people of Titchfield still hold an annual autumn 'Carnival' which processes round the streets of the town, once by daylight and once by torchlight.

> Methinks I play as I have seen them do
> In Whitsun Pastorals: sure this robe of mine
> Does change my disposition
>> (Act 4, Scene 4)

In 'The Two Gentleman of Verona' Julia (in disguise as a boy) says:

> at Pentecost,
> When all our pageants of delight were played
> Our youth got me to play the woman's part,
> And I was trimmed in Madam Julia's gown,
> As if the garment had been made for me
>> (Act 4, Scene 4)

The Whitsun Fair in Titchfield in 1592 was the background to 'Love's Labour's Lost'. We know there was also a Whitsun Service at St. Peter's Church on 14th May. The Parish Register records the Baptism of a baby boy, John Naylor.

The play is also full of references to Church Services. When the Lord's are planning their doomed retreat from the world, Berowne remarks:

> Every man with his affects [passions] is born
> Not by might mastered but by special grace

The 'special grace' is from God – and the phrase is lifted directly from the Cranmer Catechism. When Berowne, trying to pass off his perjury as an act of religion, asks 'who can sever love from charity?' he is quoting the Communion Service. Before the General Confession the Priest says, 'Ye that do truly and earnestly repent you of your sins and are in love and charity with your neighbours...' And even the Catholic Princess of France quotes the Cranmer 'Te Deum' in her reply to the King's offer of marriage:

A time, methinks, too short
To make a world-without-end bargain in.

Rosaline insults Katharine's spotty complexion by describing her as 'my red dominical, my golden letter'. The Elizabethan almanacs had red capital letters for Sundays and Feast Days. And when Rosaline mocks the folly of the Lords for dressing up as Russians ('Better wits have worn plain statute-caps') she is referring to the 'undyed woollen caps worn by people of low social rank on Sundays and Holy Days'.

A final link with the Whitsun Communion Service comes with the Masque. Dumaine attacks Holofernes, playing the role of Judas Maccabaeus, for being 'A Judas'. Holofernes counters with: 'Not Iscariot, sir'. The Gospel reading for Whitsun, from St. John's Gospel, contains the text: 'Judas saith unto him, (not Iscariot), Lord, how is it thou will manifest thyself unto us, and not unto the world?' (Chapter 14, verse15).

●

Shakespeare was riding high in May, 1592. Lord Strange had opened 'Harey the vj' (Henry VI Part One) at 'The Rose' in Southwark on the 3rd March and it was making a lot of money, though probably not for Shakespeare. But would a Whitsun service and a new play, even by a promising playwright, be enough to tempt the Earl of Essex down to Titchfield? After Rouen he was a superstar. He could always meet his friend Southampton in London; leaving the court, as he had discovered from Raleigh's plotting, was dangerous.

We know that Essex was at Richmond on 3rd May, 1592. He wrote to Lord Burghley to try to save the life of Sir John Perot, a Catholic double agent whom Elizabeth was anxious to execute. We also know he was away from court by 30th May, 1592 because Thomas Phelippes wrote to him with a message from

Elizabeth. She asks for money: Essex, in a weak hand, complies. But volatile, highly-strung and hungry for success, Essex would never be prepared, even as Guest of Honour, to be a passive spectator of Whitsun celebrations in a small Hampshire town. He was there for something far more important than a play.

●

Lines from 'Love's Labour's Lost' itself are a clue. After Berowne has insulted Boyet for colluding with the women to trick the men, Boyet ripostes:

Full merrily
Hath this brave manage, this career been run

A 'brave manage' or a 'career' was that moment in jousting when the knights' horses run at each other at full speed. Berowne makes this clear with his next line:

Lo! He is tilting straight. Peace! I have done

'Peace' or 'pax' was the cry of the knight when he acknowledged defeat in tournament.

Other clues are the magnificent portrait of the Earl of Southampton and the exquisite miniature of the Earl of Essex in the National Portrait Gallery. The men are shown, in mirrored hand-on-hip poses, showing off the same orange Devereaux tilting armour.

The clincher is a knight's helmet, dangling to this day from the ceiling in St. Peter's Church, Titchfield, said to have belonged to the 2nd Earl of Southampton. His son had arranged a Whitsun tournament to celebrate Essex's 'victory' at Rouen. Essex was down at Titchfield to 'break a lance' with friend Harry.

●

Jousting, for the Tudors, was a deadly serious business. Sir Henry Lee, at Elizabeth's Accession on 17th November, 1558, had sworn to his new Queen that he would 'present himself at the Tilt armed, the day aforesaid yearly, there to perform in honour of her sacred Majesty the promise he formerly made'. Like fairs, tournaments were ephemeral things. We have no evidence that Lee kept his word; but as he remained Queen's Champion till his retirement at the 1590 Accession Tilts, the likelihood is he did.

We know for certain there was an Accession Day tilt in Whitehall in 1577. This became the favourite spot for these annual tournaments, attended by thousands of spectators who paid a shilling each in the hope of blue-blooded carnage. There were other tournaments, of course, in Elizabeth's reign to celebrate weddings, victories or the visits of important overseas' guests. But the Accession Tilts, intended to replace Catholic Feast Days, were a unique chance for courtiers to display their prowess, loyalty, potential for military command and their taste.

It was not enough to break as many lances as possible. At each tournament a knight had to have a new 'impresa'. This comprised of a shield with a motto he presented to the Queen, a matching poem delivered by his Page (or singers) and a full theatrical 'persona', complete with costume and wig. Hermits, wild men and Indian Princes were very popular. The knight would often enter the tiltyard on a Pageant wagon, in tableau, to music. He would then change in his pavilion into a symbolic suit of armour - sending a coded message to the Queen which often completely baffled the shilling punters. Knights stuck for ideas would hire poets for the job. Even Shakespeare, three years before his early death, provided an impresa for Harry Southampton's friend, Francis Manners, Sixth Earl of Rutland – who could well have been present with his older brother at the premiere of 'Love's Labour's Lost'. Shakespeare was paid forty-four gold shillings for the job.

The Earl of Essex made his first appearance at the Accession Tilt of 1586 at the age of eighteen. A compulsive jouster, he appeared at virtually every English tournament. In 1590, the year he was made Master of the Queen's Horse, he appeared completely in black. The crowd could not work out if he was in mourning for the death of Sidney or apologising to the Queen for secretly marrying Sidney's widow. The following year Essex turned art into life at Rouen. To the amazement of the French, he thrust his lance into the town gates and offered to joust with the Governor. He wanted to prove both the rightness of his cause and the superior beauty of his mistress, Queen Elizabeth.

He had to practice tilting somewhere. In 1593 he 'rehearsed' for a week at Greenwich before the Windsor Tilts. We know from the 1737 ground plan of Titchfield Abbey that the Earl of Southampton had huge stables. Where better for Essex to practice his art than in the relative obscurity of Hampshire?

# CHAPTER 8.

# BLACK IS BEAUTIFUL

Shakespeare might have written 'Love's Labour's Lost' to Mary Southampton's commission, but he had his own agenda as well. In Sonnet 127, he writes to his infamous 'Dark Lady':

> In the old age black was not counted fair,
> Or if it were it bore not beauty's name;
> But now is black beauty's successive heir,
> And beauty slandered with a bastard shame:

*Years ago people didn't realise that 'black is beautiful'. Or if they did, they didn't put the two words together. The word 'black' has now taken over from the word 'beauty'. 'Beauty' is the word that is now abused.*

> For since each hand hath put on Nature's power,
> Fairing the foul with Art's false borrow'd face,
> Sweet beauty hath no name, no holy bower,
> But is profaned, if not lives in disgrace.

*Women now defy nature by using cosmetics to hide their ugliness. Beauty has lost its reputation and its sanctity. It has not been totally disgraced, but it has certainly been vulgarised.*

> Therefore my Mistress' eyes are raven black,
> Her brows so suited, and they mourners seem
> At such who, not born fair, no beauty lack,
> Sland'ring Creation with a false esteem;

*Your eyes and brows are black like ravens because they are in mourning for women, not born beautiful, who snatch their so-called 'beauty' from Nature and so demean it.*

> Yet so they mourn, becoming of their woe,
> That every tongue says beauty should look so.

*But you look so gorgeous, dressed up all in black for their funeral, that there's not a man in the world who does not say: 'Black is beautiful.'*

Berowne uses identical language in 'Love's Labour's Lost' when the King accuses Rosaline of being 'black as ebony':

> Is ebony like her? O word divine!
> A wife of such wood were felicity.
> O, who can give an oath, where is a book?
> That I may swear beauty doth beauty lack
> If that she learn not of her eye to look.
> No face is fair that is not full so black...

*Does ebony resemble her? Then it is a wood graced by God – and to be married to a woman made out of it would be the highest happiness. I want to make a vow – has anyone got a Bible? I want to swear that women who seem beautiful have no beauty at all unless they are black-eyed like my love.*

The King insists that black is a colour fit only for Hell, dungeons and deepest night; but Berowne triumphantly asserts that:

> If in black my lady's brows be decked,
> It mourns that painting and usurping hair
> Should ravish doters with a false aspect;
> And therefore is she born to make black fair.
> Her favour turns the fashion of the days,
> For native blood is counted painting now:
> And therefore red, that would avoid dispraise,
> Paints itself black, to imitate her brow

*My lady's eyebrows are black because they mourn the fact that artificial cosmetics and wigs can dazzle love-sick men. The whole purpose of her existence is to make black beautiful – and because she is so gorgeous she has created a new fashion. Women with naturally red cheeks now look made-up: so, to avoid being criticised, they plaster themselves with black cosmetics to mimic my lady's black brows.*

In Sonnet 130 Shakespeare teases the Dark Lady:

> I love to hear her speak, yet well I know
> That Music hath a far more pleasing sound;
> I grant I never saw a goddess go;
> My mistress when she walks treads on the ground.

*I love your voice – but music sounds better. It's true I have never seen a Goddess walk. But when you walk, the earth knows all about it.*

Berowne teases Rosaline in the same way when he describes her in his poem as 'the fairest goddess on the ground'. And the bantering tone of Sonnet 130 is echoed by Berowne's horrified amazement, in his soliloquy, that he has fallen in love with -

> A woman that is like a German clock,
> Still a-repairing, ever out of frame
> And never going aright, being a watch,
> But being watched that it may still go right!

*A woman that is like a clock made in Germany: always needing repairs, always breaking down, never keeping the right time – and never behaving itself properly unless you keep a constant eye on it.*

Berowne is first of a line of Shakespeare's characters, cynical, but compassionate outsiders, Mercutio, Benedick, Puck, Jacques, Hamlet, Enobarbus and even Falstaff, who seem, at times, to speak for Shakespeare himself.

Shakespeare speaks for himself most clearly in his Sonnets; but it is important to realise that their publication in 1609 was a slip-shod, mysterious affair which Shakespeare did not oversee. The compositors constantly misread 'their' for 'thy' so clearly had no understanding of their meaning. All the sonnets to 'the lovely boy' are at the beginning, and all those basically to the 'Dark Lady' are at the back. But life does not categorise itself so simply, and the Sonnets, apart from the opening set of seventeen, are not printed in the order of their composition. Some, I hope to show, were written as late as 1604. But the sonnets to the Dark Lady, from their language, imagery and thought, are clearly contemporaneous with the first production of 'Love's Labour's Lost' in 1592.

Shakespeare concludes Sonnet 136 with 'my name is Will'. He has been playing on the pun between his own name, and the Elizabethan word for penis. (In England, at least, little boys still have their 'willies'). He starts the sonnet to the Dark Lady with:

> If thy soul check thee that I come so near,
> Swear to thy blind soul that I was thy Will,
> And will, thy soul knows, is admitted there.

*If you do not care for me personally, then pretend I am not Will Shakespeare, but simply a 'Willie'. You know you love 'Willies' even if you don't love 'Will'.*

When the King of Navarre tells the Princess of the vow the men have made, she says 'Why will shall break it, will and nothing else'. She is making a joke about the sexual drives of the men; but there is another 'in-joke'. Shakespeare himself, I believe, played Berowne. With limited resources and rehearsal time at Titchfield, Shakespeare could ensure a certain level of performance by giving himself most of the work. Berowne/Will is certainly the first to break his oath in the play. By casting himself as Berowne, Shakespeare promotes himself to the aristocracy as 'a merry madcap Lord' and declares his love by proxy, at this time of May madness, to the Dark Lady herself.

Like old time variety artists, who never gave their acts away to their fellow-performers, he probably kept his great speeches a secret till the 'first night'.*

---

* Actors in Shakespeare's day – and indeed for centuries later – were only given their cue lines in their scripts.

●

In 1597 one Emilia Lanier, née Bassano (1569-1645), paid several visits to the famous astrologer, Simon Forman (1552-1611), who had fixed a favourable date for Queen Elizabeth's Accession. From his notes we learn that Emilia 'had hard fortune in her youth' because her father who was 'miserable in his estate' had 'died when she was young'. Brought up by the Countess of Kent, she had 'been favoured much of Her Majesty and many noblemen, and has had great gifts and been much made of'. She became mistress to the bluff old soldier Lord Hunsdon, the Lord Chamberlain, who 'married her in money and jewels' and gave her an allowance of £40 a year. But she fell pregnant, and though she had often had abortions, she was married to the 'minstrel' Alphonse Lanier 'for colour'.

By the time she consulted Forman her husband had 'dealt hardly with her' and had 'spent and consumed her goods'. She was so hard-up and in so much debt, she was thinking of becoming a 'good fellow' (a prostitute). Lanier was about to join Essex's Islands Voyage to the Azores 'in hope to be knighted' and Emilia went to Forman to find out 'whether she should be a lady or no'. Forman later observes that Lanier 'was not knighted, nor yet worthy thereof'. He called on Emilia, who could 'hardly keep secret', at her house on 20th September and 'felt all parts of her body willingly and kissed her often, but she would not do in any wise'. Not surprisingly, Emilia 'dealt evil with him after...'

A.L. Rowse (1904-1997), from whom these quotations were taken, was the first to discover that Emilia was the Dark Lady of the Sonnets. He rushed too quickly into print in an article in 'The Times' in 1973, made some slips and was crucified by the English academic establishment. But he was essentially right. The Bassano family, a group of black Sephardic Jewish musicians, composers and instrument-makers, originally from

North Africa, but settled in the town of Bassano near Venice, was well known to the Southamptons. Harry's grandfather Thomas, the 1st Earl, (the sadist with the musical ear) had heard the Bassanos play at a dinner given by Queen Mary of Hungary in Brussels in February, 1539. He wrote to Thomas Cromwell that they were 'the fineliest I ever have heard'. The Bassanos had visited Henry VIII's court in 1531: but after the 1st Earl's letter, they came to live in England permanently, though keeping their links with Venice. King Henry, turning a blind eye to the fact they were Jewish and so forbidden entry to England, gave them a dissolved monastery in London's East End for their home. In a flash these Jewish Roman Catholics became Jewish Protestants.

Emilia Bassano was the youngest daughter of Baptista Bassano and his 'reputed wife Margaret Bassany alias Johnson'. When Shakespeare, in Sonnet 127, writes -

> But now is black beauty's successive heir
> And beauty slandered with a bastard shame

- he is teasing Emilia because her parents, both then dead, were not married.

We know the Dark Lady was a musician. In Sonnet 128 Shakespeare envies the wooden keys of the virginals 'that nimble leap,/To kiss the tender inward of thy hand'. In Sonnet 134 he makes fun of her selective promiscuity and her Jewishness:

> The statute of thy beauty thou wilt take,
> Thou usurer, that put'st forth all to use

*You will take every single thing you can get with your beauty – you money-lender who lends everything to everyone.*

Jewish people were forced to resort to illegal money-lending as a way of survival: the Dark Lady is presented as a usurer who gives everything she has to anyone who asks. In Sonnet 137 Shakespeare describes her as 'the bay where all men ride': and in Sonnet 139 begs her not to eye up other men when they are together:

> But in my sight,
> Dear heart, forbear to glance thine eye aside.

In Sonnet 135 Shakespeare plays on the word 'will' again. In Shakespeare's time 'will' could refer to the female sex organ as well:

> Wilt thou, whose will is large and spacious,
> Not once vouchsafe to hide my will in thine?
> Shall will in others seem right gracious
> And in my will no fair acceptance shine?

*Will you, with your massive pudenda, not allow me access to it with my penis? Will you always find other men's penises more attractive than mine?*

Berowne makes the same joke to Rosaline in 'Love's Labour's Lost':

> Your capacity
> Is of that nature that to your huge store
> Wise things seem foolish and rich things but poor.

If we take the current dating of 'Love's Labour's Lost'- 1594 - we have a problem. The pregnant Emilia Bassano became Emilia Lanier on 18th October, 1592 at St. Botolph's, Aldgate. Her son would have been in his 'terrible twos' when the play was first produced. The promiscuous behaviour of the Dark Lady does not suggest a married woman with a toddler in tow: the darkest of ladies will transform into the most caring of mothers. In Sonnet 143 Shakespeare describes himself in his relation to the Dark Lady as a baby whom 'a careful housewife' puts down to run after an escaping chicken. He would never have used that image if a real baby had been involved.

Roger Prior, who with David Lasocki,* did brilliant back-up research to Rowse's theory, believes that Shakespeare was pursuing a married woman. His evidence is Sonnet 152:

> In loving thee thou know'st I am forsworn
> But thou art twice forsworn to me love swearing,
> In act thy bed-vow broke and new faith torn,
> In vowing new hate after new love bearing.

*I'm a married man. When I sleep with you, you know very well that I am breaking my marriage vows. But when you say you love me, you break your vows twice over. One to your old lover that you wouldn't sleep with anyone else – and one to your new lover when you tell me now you hate me.*

Emilia's 'bed-vow' is not a wedding vow, like Shakespeare's. It refers to Emilia's mock marriage with Lord Hunsdon who 'married her in money and jewels'. Hunsdon needed to keep her faithful to preserve his health.

In May, 1592, Emilia Bassano, like Rosaline in the play, was unmarried. (Berowne asks Boyet of Rosaline: 'Is she wedded or no?'. Boyet replies; 'To her will sir, or so'.) Hunsdon was not only a powerful figure politically: as Lord Chamberlain he also chose the plays for court. But he was not to become patron to Shakespeare's company till 1594. Even Shakespeare might have thought twice about going to bed with the boss's girlfriend.

Emilia's presence in Hampshire is easily explained. Lord Montague employed the Bassanos ('her Highnesse musicians') to provide the music for the Queen's deer shoot at Cowdray. But, more important, Hunsdon was at the 1591 Privy Council meetings on 20th August at Cowdray, 3rd September at Titchfield and 22nd September at Farnham near Elvetham. Away from his wife in London, Hunsdon, nearly 70, (who was

---

* *The Bassanos,* (1995)

said to take as much delight in hanging 'Scotch thieves' as other men take in hawking and hunting) would have had his expensive, twenty-one year old mistress with him. She was a favourite of the Queen and could join in with the entertainment, just as she had done in her youth with the Countess of Kent at Cookham.

Mary Southampton, a woman of the world and in dire need of the favour of the Privy Council, could well have offered Hunsdon and Emilia the privacy of Whiteley Lodge, last out-post of the hated Dymock, two discreet miles away from 'Place House' itself.

This would explain why Berowne in the play describes the dark-skinned Rosaline as:

> A whiteley wanton with a velvet brow
> With two pitch balls stuck in her face for eyes

Emilia, I believe, was also present at the first performance of 'Love's Labour's Lost'. It would be natural for Emilia's family to provide the music for this event, as they had done at Cowdray. Emilia herself might even have written the music for the songs.

●

Costard, in the play, directly refers to Moth as 'My sweet ounce of man's flesh, my incony [beloved] Jew'. Editors, from Alexander Pope (1688-1744) up to the present, have performed double somersaults to prove that 'Jew' does not mean 'Jew'. It is short for 'jewel' or even 'Juvenal'. But Samuel Johnson (1709-1784) thought that 'Jew' should stand: 'I know not whether it be right, however specious, to change Jew for Jewel. Jew in our author's time, was, for whatever reason, apparently a word of endearment.'

It was a word of 'endearment' because the boy playing Moth was also, I believe, a member of the Bassano family. He is called

Moth in reference to his size and the dark tone of his skin. When Don Armado asks him to 'warble', Shakespeare writes just one word: 'Concolinel'. This was clearly a song in the repertoire of the musicians, known also to the boy.

There happens to be a member of the Bassano family who was twelve in 1592: Anthony Bassano, the only one of Arthur Bassano's children who grew up to be a musician.* Arthur Bassano had married an English woman, Margaret Lothbury, who could well have been a singer. Just before Moth recites a poem to Don Armado, he says 'My father's wit and my mother's tongue assist me'. I believe he is referring to a sung under-scoring to the poem provided by Arthur and Margaret 'Bassany'. The casting of Anthony in such a quick-witted, sympathetic rôle would have delighted the Bassanos. They would also have roared with laughter as Shakespeare, enumerating Rosaline/Emilia's faults, made reluctant love to a boy player in black-face. As Italian speakers from Venice, they would also have relished the pedant Holfernes' line: 'Venetia, Venetia, Chi non ti vede, non ti pretia' ('Venice, Venice: who has not seen thee does not know thy worth'). Shows often include jokes for the band.

But if Shakespeare wrote 'Love's Labour's Lost' for Titchfield in 1592, why didn't he write the Queen's Progress Entertainment at Cowdray the previous year?

Perhaps he did.

---

* Anthony Bassano ended up making cornets, crumhorns and Royal recorders. At the age of 24 he helped to provide the 'loud music' at Queen Elizabeth's funeral. Perhaps he also gave the off-stage trumpet call in 'Love's Labour's Lost' that announces the arrival of the Masquers.

# CHAPTER 9

# THE CHARGE-HOUSE
# UPON THE MOUNTAIN

In the Cowdray Progress a comic porter greets Queen Elizabeth. As every schoolboy knows, a comic porter appears in 'Macbeth'. But, more important, there are characteristic words and phrases in the Cowdray Progress that Shakespeare uses in his plays and poems.

The Porter refers to Elizabeth as 'the world's wonder': the King of Navarre says: 'Navarre shall be the wonder of the world' (Act 1, Scene 1).

The Pilgrim describes Elizabeth as 'fairest of all creatures': the first sonnet of Shakespeare begins: 'From fairest creatures we desire increase'.

The Wild Man describes the sea as 'rampired with true hearts invincible'. In 'Timon of Athens' the First Senator says, 'Set but thy foot/Against our rampired gates, and they shall ope.' (Act 5, Scene 4).

The Wild Man talks about Elizabeth's 'clemency': the Actors in Hamlet beg their audience for the same favour:

> For us and for our tragedy,
> Here stooping to your clemency,
> We beg your hearing patiently.
>
> (Act 3, Scene 2).

The Angler talks about 'this nibbling world'. Touchstone in 'As You Like It' says 'as pigeons bill, so wedlock would be nibbling' (Act 3, Scene3) and the Goddess Iris in 'The Tempest' talks about Ceres 'turfy mountains where live nibbling sheep' (Act 4, Scene 1).

The Angler says, 'The sun so glisters that the fish see my hook through the bait'. In 'Venus and Adonis' it is the eye of a lustful stallion 'which scornfully glisters like fire/Shows his hot courage and his high desire' (ll. 274-5).

The Fisherman refers to 'hollow hearts'. So does Queen Katharine in 'King Henry VIII': 'But cardinal sins and hollow hearts I fear ye' (Act 3, Scene 1).

The Fisherman describes some of Elizabeth's subjects as 'muddy-minded', preferring to live 'in a standing pool'. This is very close to Hamlet's self-laceration in Act 2, Scene 2:

> Yet I
> A dull and muddy-mettled rascal, peak
> Like John-a-dreams, unpregnant of my cause.

And Edgar, disguised as Poor Tom, 'drinks the green mantle of the standing pool' (King Lear, Act 3, Scene 4).

Most important of all, the Pilgrim describes the Wild Man he has encountered as a 'rough-hewed ruffian'. One of the most loved lines from 'Hamlet' runs:

> There's a divinity that shapes our ends,
> Rough-hew them how we will
> (Act 5, Scene 2).

This final touch proves that Shakespeare wrote the Cowdray Progress. Or does it?

●

There was a contemporary of Shakespeare's who used the verb 'rough-hew' at least twice in his work. His father, 'Hebrew in blood but not in faith', claimed to be a Franciscan monk from Florence who had converted to Protestantism and narrowly escaped a death-cell in Rome. After a breathless flight through Europe (ditching his monk's habit in Apulia) he finally ended up in England in 1550, three years into the Protestant reign of Edward VI. Granted an annuity of £20 a year by Burghley (probably for spying) he became language tutor to Lady Jane Grey and vicar of an Italian Church in London. He impregnated a woman and married her. When Catholic Mary came to the throne, he was off again with his wife and one year old son to Soglio in the Grison cantons of Switzerland, a haven for Italian Protestants fleeing from persecution. His wife was probably English (his son was later described as 'An English stock but an Italian plant') and most probably a Londoner. Given the circumstances of the marriage, and his son's later mastery of street argot, she was probably part of the City's 'low-life'.

Their son, aged twenty-three, returned to England in 1576, safely into Elizabeth's Protestant reign. Probably never having set foot in Italy, possibly with a thick Cockney accent, he set himself up as 'Giovanni' the Master of Italian culture. Or, if it better suited his purposes, 'The Resolute John Florio'.

As a language teacher, he had to be the genuine article; but the Tudor English hated foreigners. So he assumed a double persona: he presented himself as 'an Englishman in Italian'. He matriculated from Magdalene College, Oxford, as a poor scholar in 1581. From 1583 he spent some time as a language tutor to the daughter of the French Ambassador. Like his father before him, he was probably a spy, placed there by Burghley to keep an eye on correspondence with Mary, Queen of Scots.

In 1578 Florio published 'First Fruits', ostensibly an Italian language manual, but in reality a blatant act of self-promotion. Dedicated to Dudley, Earl of Leicester, it begins with a series of commendatory verses from satisfied clients, then goes on to table Italian and English conversations, side by side. In these Florio projects himself as an Italian who arrived in England knowing no English but who has mastered the language perfectly in a single year. What he has done for himself in English, he can do for you in Italian. It will only take three months to be word-perfect – at half the rate the French teachers are charging. The mongrel language English is useless beyond Dover. You can only become a fully civilised gentleman of the world if you study Italian. And you study it with Giovanni.

This book would be of little interest to us except for one remarkable fact: Shakespeare knew it backwards. The first phrase that leaps from its pages is Florio's translation of the Italian phrase 'Tutto quelche luce, non é ora': 'All that glistereth is not gold'. This is followed by: 'We need not speak so much of love, all books are full of love, with so many authors, that it were labour lost to speak of love'. It culminates in: 'Venetia, chi no ti vede, non ti pretia', the very phrase Holofernes uses.

Florio also compiled 'A World of Words', an Italian / English Dictionary dedicated to Roger Manners, 5th Earl of Rutland (Southampton's young friend), the 3rd Earl himself and the Countess of Bedford. It was published in 1598: but in 1591, Florio wrote he had made great progress with his work and would 'shortly send into the world an exquisite Italian and English dictionary and a compendious grammar'.

Florio translates *abbozzare* as: 'To rough-hew or cast any first draft, to bungle up ill-favouredly.' In his translation of the Essays of Montaigne (published 1603) one passage runs: 'My consultation doth somewhat roughly hew the matter. The main and chief points of the work I am wont to resign to heaven'.

From the 1598 dedication to his dictionary we know that Florio had been in 'the pay and patronage' of Southampton 'for some years'. But we also know that in 1594 John Florio was definitely at Titchfield. He and Southampton's barber threatened to throw the Sheriff of Southampton overboard from the Itchen ferry for meddling in Southampton family business. The Sheriff had the audacity to try to arrest the Danvers brothers, friends of the 3rd Earl, for a murder in Wiltshire.

Florio did not call himself 'The Resolute' for nothing.

●

Dame Frances Yates (1900-1981) was the first to suggest Burghley placed Florio in Titchfield as a spy. His 'front' was to be Italian tutor to Southampton: but Burghley would most likely have insisted that a Protestant taught the impressionable young Titchfield schoolboys as well. So Florio, backed by 'the State', pushed Shakespeare out of his job. I believe Mary Southampton, championing Shakespeare, kept him on in her household (much as she had kept Swithin Wells) as a 'generally nice person to have around'. Shakespeare's characterisation of Berowne in 'Love's Labour's Lost', part of the group, but slightly aside, witty, inventive and self-mocking, was very much the rôle Shakespeare himself played in the Titchfield household.

One of the advantages of losing the schoolmaster's job was that Mary, and later, her son, started to pay him for his writing. In his dedication to 'Venus and Adonis' Shakespeare vows 'to take advantage of all idle hours' to write another poem which suggests he had a 'day-job' as well. It would also have given him more time to continue to write song lyrics, interludes and entertainments for the household.

'A Comedy of Errors', very much in the Christianised Roman tradition of 'Ralph Roister Doister', was probably written for a Christmas schoolboy performance in the Hall at Titchfield. The play, which has references to cold weather, requires an upper entrance ('The Place' had a minstrels' gallery), contains a vivid description of another greasy kitchen maid and names what could be further members of the

Southampton household (Maud, Bridget, Marian, Cicely, Gillian and Ginn). At one point Dromio of Syracuse enters, in the needless stage direction, 'from the bay', suggesting Shakespeare had the Titchfield topography in his unconscious. At another point the same character describes France as 'armed and reverted, making war against her heir' which could well be another reference to the campaign of Henri of Navarre.

Strangely, 'Pericles', currently placed as a late work but thought by John Dryden (1631-1700) to be Shakespeare's first,* provides a companion piece. In both plays the protagonists lose wives who re-appear at Ephesus, one as an Abbess in the monastery, and one as a Priestess at the Temple of Diana. In both there is a background of storms at sea (the Solent is notoriously treacherous for shipping), harbours and brothels – and the coffin of Pericles' wife is washed ashore like flotsam and gettson. Certainly the sea – and the importance of the sea-coast - as a generator of spiritual transformation was to return time and again in Shakespeare's plays.

●

Mary probably wanted Shakespeare to write the Cowdray Progress: but it was her father's entertainment. Father and daughter both needed to appease Lord Burghley, Burghley had appointed Florio, so Florio got the job. Shakespeare was experiencing at first hand how 'art' could be made 'tongue-tied by authority' (Sonnet 66).

---

* He writes:  *Shakespeare's* own Muse her *Pericles* first bore
The prince of *Tyre* was elder than the *Moor:*
Tis a miracle to see a first good play,
All Hawthorns do not bloom on Christmas-day *Miscellany Poems* (1684)
Perhaps 'Pericles' was an early play Shakespeare revised in his maturity.

Florio, though, had much that Shakespeare needed. He was intimate with Italian literature and customs. He had a library of Italian novellas and plays. He was, in his translation of Montaigne, opening advanced European thought to 'backward' England. Most important of all, he was 'inventing' new English words. Although he affected to despise English, by the time he published his Dictionary he had changed his mind. He realised that the English vocabulary was richer than the Italian and wrote in his Preface that 'it must be a pleasure to them [Englishmen] to see so rich a tongue [Italian] out-vied by their Mother speech'. Florio, to gain patronage, would have needed to show his 'work in progress' to Southampton: Southampton would have shown it to Shakespeare; Shakespeare plundered it. He might never have used the phrase 'rough-hew' in 'Hamlet' if Florio had not used it first.

The writer of the Cowdray Progress creates the character of the Pilgrim who declares he has 'travelled many countries'. Florio's habit was to cast himself as a Traveller, refined and cultivated in the ways of the world. Holofernes, as he quotes the Venetia phrase in 'Love's Labour's Lost', declares: 'I may speak of thee as the Traveller speaks of Venice...'

The Pilgrim was a perfect part for Florio to play to show his wit and his loyalty to the Queen, in the same way Holofernes performs the part of Judas Maccabaeus in the Masque he has written for the Princess of France. Frances Yates quotes the Welsh poet and colonist, Sir William Vaughan (1575-1641) who, in 'The Spirit of Detraction' (1611), complains that if 'an ingenuous scholar...but broach forth the barrel of his wit, which God hath given him; they cry out his brain is an empty barrel, his wit but barren, his matter borrowed out of other mens' books'. Later, in 'The Golden Fleece'(1626), Vaughan names the 'ingenuous scholar' as his friend John Florio.

It was Florio who broached forth 'the barrel of his wit' by writing and acting in the Cowdray Progress. It is Shakespeare who cries out that Florio's 'brain is an empty barrel, his wit barren and his matter borrowed out of other men's books' by sending him up in 'Love's Labour's Lost' as Holofernes the pedant. William Warburton (1698-1779), the Bishop of Gloucester, in his 1747 edition of Shakespeare, writes that 'By Holofernes is designed a particular character, a pedant and schoolmaster of our Author's time, one John Florio, a teacher of the Italian tongue in London.'

Many scholars have pointed out that Holofernes talks like Florio's Dictionary. He describes the deer that the Princess shoots as being 'ripe as the pomewater [a whitish apple], who now hangeth like a jewel in the ear of coelo, the sky, the welkin, the heaven.' Florio, in his 'World of Words', defines 'caelo' as 'heaven, the sky, the firmament or welkin.' Holofernes, when he improvises a poem to celebrate the Princess's shooting of the deer, uses exaggerated alliteration: 'The preyful princess pierc'd and prick'd a pretty pleasing pricket'. So does Florio: 'Proverbs' he writes, 'are the pith, the proprieties, the proofs, the purities of language'.

Writers, in my experience of commissioning scripts, always base their characters on people they know. They may mix people together, throw in aspects of themselves and even try to enter the minds of distant 'celebrities' or historical figures. But they also try to give their creations a life of their own.

Holofernes has life in abundance. He is himself chock full of the faults he projects onto the vain Don Armado: 'His humour is lofty, his discourse peremptory, his tongue filed, his eye ambitious, his gait majestical, and his general behaviour vain, ridiculous and thrasonical [boastful].' But Shakespeare not only gives him a life: he gives him a soul. Holofernes redeems himself by inviting the illiterate Constable Dull to dinner with his pupil's father. And when the young Lords heckle him as he plays Judas Maccabaeus, he is brave, even 'resolute': 'This is not generous, not gentle, not humble'.

Years later, as Bishop Warburton points out, Florio was to have his own revenge on Shakespeare in the Preface to his Dictionary. It is unclear how many people he attacks or who they are: but when he writes - 'Let Aristophanes and his comedians make plays and scour their mouths on Socrates; those very mouths they make to vilify, shall be the means to amplify his virtue' - it is clear he had Shakespeare in mind

●

But what did Shakespeare have in mind when Don Armado says to Holofernes: 'Do you not educate youth at the charge-house upon the top of the mountain?'. And Holofernes replies: 'Or, mons, the hill.'? The lines have bamboozled Shakespearean scholars since they started to edit his works two hundred and fifty years ago.

Mountain is spelt 'Mountaine' in the original printing. I believe this is a joking reference to Florio's translation of Montaine. 'The hill' is most likely a rude joke about the 'mons Veneris' (the 'Hill of Venus' in women): but it also refers to the incline down to Titchfield Town from 'Place House'.

But the big question is what Shakespeare means by 'charge-house'. Some scholars think 'charge-house' means 'a free school', others a 'school that charges fees'. Some think it is a school where pupils are taken 'in charge' at the cost of the Parish. The latest Arden edition quotes the Oxford English Dictionary: 'house for the charging, filling up or burdening of youth, a school': but the only citation of the word in the Dictionary is from 'Love's Labour's Lost' itself. Some editors pass over the problem in silence. Some admit they just do not know.

I found the 'charge-house' by chance. Because the Grammar School that Leland mentioned was so crucial to my research, I visited Titchfield again to see if I could find any foundations by 'the banks' of the 'river', now a canal since the 3rd Earl built his notorious sea-wall. There was nothing.

Disappointed, I turned to houses erected on the spot where the Grammar School might have been – where a building is shown in the early Jacobean map of Titchfield. There was a row of cottages. One of them had a note stuck in the window:

'Old Grammar School'

It never occurred to me it could still be standing. Shaking with excitement, I tried to take photographs. The owner saw me outside and kindly invited me in. He had become interested in the medieval history of his own beautiful home at about the same time that I began my work on 'Love's Labour's Lost'.* He showed me a medieval wall in his kitchen and told me that Dendro dating of roof-timbers had revealed the house had been built in 1447/8. This was the year Henry VI granted the Fair, and economic favours, to Titchfield. He could well have endowed a grammar school as well.

There were, the owner said, Tudor additions of around 1550. He showed me a fireplace in the schoolroom where schoolboys had stamped their initials into the green oak. The end section of the cottage and the whole upper storey was Tudor. 'There's an interesting feature in our bedroom' he said, guiding me up the stairs.

Interesting feature....

Standing before me were the remains, to the ceiling, of a

---

* Ken Groves, who has since become a good friend and has shared his genealogical researches with me freely.

secure partition with wooden bars, like a bank or a prison. This was clearly 'the charge-house' where 'Holofernes' educated youth. But what was it?

To begin with I thought it might be the place where tenants came to pay their rents to the Titchfield schoolmaster who doubled as 'cashier'. Or perhaps where the hundred-man entourage of the 2nd Earl would have called for its wages and rations. But the 1737 groundplan shows an audit room in 'Place House' itself. To this day 'a charge-house' can be a secure place where gun-powder is stored. In the scene in which the 'charge-house' is mentioned in 'Love's Labour's Lost' (Act 5, Scene 1), fireworks, to amuse the Princess of France as they amused Elizabeth at Elvetham, are also discussed. But would volatile gun-powder have been stored in the upper room of a school-house, even by the highly eccentric Southamptons?

The original partition would have blocked the present window – so the charge-house, with its bars, might originally have been dark. Then I remembered the 'hungry lean-fac'd villain' Pinch, the exorcist in 'The Comedy of Errors'. In the stage directions Shakespeare calls him 'a schoolmaster': but in the text he is named only as a 'conjurer'. Pinch declares Antipholus of Ephesus possessed – and orders that, like Malvolio in 'Twelfth Night', he must be 'bound and laid in some dark room'. He tries to 'cure' Antipholus by banishing the Devil from him:

> I charge thee, Satan, hous'd within this man,
> To yield possession to my holy prayers,
> And to thy state of darkness hie thee straight;
> I conjure thee by all the saints in heaven.
>
> (Act 4, Scene 4)

The editor of the Arden edition of the play, pointing out that 'the word conjure = solemnly charge, is the proper one for an exorcist to use', draws a parallel with the dialogue of Antipholus of Syracuse to the Courtesan in the scene before:

'Satan avoid, I charge thee, tempt me not'.

Schoolmasters could speak Latin, so were thought to be able to converse with spirits*.

In the days of Titchfield Abbey, the monks would have cared for the insane, as the Abbess does in 'The Comedy of Errors'. But after the Dissolution, the Titchfield schoolmaster must have taken on the role of exorcist. Shakespeare, a believer but not a fanatical believer, mocks this dark aspect of Catholicism.

When Feste, disguised as a priest, comes to visit Malvolio in the 'dark-room', he says: 'Peace in this prison'.

The barred structure above the Titchfield Grammar School could have been the place where lunatics and criminals were kept in darkness. And where Satan, 'housed' in the souls of the insane, was 'charged' to depart by the proselytising Catholic schoolmaster who held the position in Titchfield before Shakespeare – Swithin Wells.

---

* In 'Hamlet' the soldiers on the battlements ask Horatio to 'question' the ghost because he is 'a scholar'.

# CHAPTER 10.

# BY SPIRITS TAUGHT TO WRITE

When the Lords are arguing whose mistress is the most beautiful, Berowne makes his claim that 'No face is fair that is not full so black' as Rosaline's. The King of Navarre responds with:

> O paradox! Black is the badge of Hell.
> The hue of dungeons and the school of night

To this day the phrase 'The School of Night' unleashes vengeful controversy in the academic world. Eighteenth century scholars, even Malone, amended 'school' to 'scowl'. Some scholars insist it simply means the place where night learnt to be black.

But others suggest Satanic goings-on. They relate 'The School of Night' to the 'School of Atheism', the group of wild-living, ambi-sexual free-thinkers, including Marlowe, who were said to surround Raleigh at Durham House in London.

'The School of Night' really existed. But it was pretentious rather than demonic. And some of its members were Titchfield neighbours.

In 1594 George Chapman (c.1559-1634) dedicated 'The Shadow of Night', an obscure mystical work, praising cool, rational night over hot, lustful day, to 'My dear and most worthy friend Mathew Roydon'. A typical extract runs:

> All you possessed with indepressed [aspiring] spirits
> Endued with nimble and inspiring wits,
> Come consecrate with me, to sacred night
> Your whole endeavours and detest the light....
> No pen can anything eternal write
> That is not steep'd in humour of the night.

For Chapman, the moon, synonymous with Queen Elizabeth, was superior to the Sun. In 'Hymnus in Cynthiam' (Hymn to Cynthia) Chapman explicitly exhorts the Queen to do nothing so vulgar as to marry a sunlit European Prince:

> Then set thy crystal and imperial throne
> (Girt in thy chaste, and never loosing zone)
> 'Gainst Europe's Sun, directly opposite
> And give him darkness that doth threat thy light.

Roydon was not the only dedicatee: the others were 'that most ingenious Derby, deep-searching Northumberland, and skill embracing heir of Hunsdon'.

'Most ingenious Derby' by 1594 was the 5th Earl of Derby, Ferdinando, Lord Strange (c.1559-1594), Mary Southampton's cousin and Shakespeare's theatre Patron.

'Deep-searching Northumberland' was 'the Wizard Earl', Henry Percy (1564-1632), who lived at nearby Petworth. Infatuated with Catholicism, science, astronomy and tobacco, with the political embarrassment of an uncle who had been executed after the Northern Rebellion, he was forbidden by Elizabeth to travel more than thirty miles from his home. Titchfield was within that range.

The 'heir of Hunsdon' was Sir George Carey (c.1556-1617), son of Lord Hunsdon, Emilia Bassano's 'keeper'. He had been appointed Captain of the strategically vital Isle of Wight in 1582. So he was a Titchfield neighbour as well.

In his dedication to 'Ovid's Banquet of Sense', Chapman, making clear his hatred of 'the profane multitude', consecrates his 'strange poems to those searching spirits, whom learning hath made noble, and nobility sacred'. 'The School of Night' was the nick-name for Chapman's local aristocratic dedicatees who, with more money than sense, funded his snobby, abstruse philosophical outpourings.

Strange, Northumberland and Carey knew Chapman, Chapman knew Roydon and Roydon knew Raleigh. Northumberland was also a great friend of Sir Walter: he ended up in the Tower with him in the reign of James VI and I. The Wizard Earl had such a high old time there, constructing bowling alleys, designing sundials and talking philosophy with Raleigh, that he did not want to go back to his wife. Yates has found an essay by the Earl on the incompatibility of the love of women and the love of study – a theme, she points out, Shakespeare takes up in 'Love's Labour's Lost'. Raleigh had a loose association with this group of men: but was far too bright to be on Chapman's subscription list.

John Nichols (1745-1826), the compiler of the magisterial 'Progresses and Public Processions of Queen Elizabeth', quotes Dallaway who says 'it is certain Queen Elizabeth stayed at Petworth' in her 1591 Progress to the South-East. The Wizard Earl would have invited the other 'searching spirits' to his home to celebrate 'Cynthia'. Chapman might even have recited his 'Hymnus in Cynthiam' to the Queen in person. Every sympathy would be with Her Majesty.

Raleigh, invited as a friend of Northumberland, would have continued to rubbish Essex to the Queen. And if the Montague/Southamptons had been invited, as they most certainly were, 'The School' could have tried to recruit the teenage Lord Harry.

Chapman was certainly working on him...

●

Chapman was a psychic who had been possessed by the soul of Homer in the most unlikely of places:

'I am' said he 'that spirit Elysian
That in thy native air and on the hill
Next Hitchin's left hand, did thy bosom fill...'

Shakespeare, in Sonnet 78, complains of a rival poet who wants to replace him in Harry's affections:

So oft have I invoked thee for my Muse
And found such fair assistance in my verse
As every alien pen hath got my use
And under thee their poesy disperse.

*I have so often called upon you, Harry, for inspiration, and found such beautiful help with my writing, that every other poet is imitating me – and using you to enhance their verse.*

Thine eyes, that taught the dumb on high to sing
And heavy ignorance aloft to fly,
Have added feathers to the learned's wing,
And given grace a double Majesty.

*Your eyes that allowed someone as inarticulate as I was to write good verse – and someone handicapped as me by lack of a formal education to fulfil himself – now give the same help to people already educated – and extra culture to the already cultured.*

Yet be most proud of that which I compile,
Whose influence is thine, and born of thee:
In other's works thou dost but mend the style,
And Arts, with thy sweet graces, graced be;

*But you should be most proud of the verses I write – that have their very origins in you. You might help other writers to improve their style – and sweeten their verse with the sweetness of your personality.*

But thou art all my art, and dost advance
As high as learning, my rude ignorance.

*But you are my sole inspiration; you transform my illiteracy into erudition.*

Shakespeare here, honestly admitting that he has no formal education, claims he has been inspired to write by the personality of Southampton alone. The rival poet is a University man: Southampton simply enhances a learning that was already in place. In Shakespeare's case, Southampton actually creates the scholarship. He transmutes, by his very being, Shakespeare's 'rude ignorance'. Shakespeare hits nearer home with Sonnet 86:

> Was it his spirit, by spirits taught to write
> Above a mortal pitch, that struck me dead?
> No, neither he, nor his compeers by night
> Giving him aid, my verse astonished.

*Was it his inspiration – doubly inspired by the help of dead poets like Homer – that made him write verse that no mortal could achieve unaided, verse that killed my creative spirit? No, it wasn't him – nor the peers, whom he considers his equals, who subsidise his verse - who inhibited mine.*

> He, nor that affable familiar ghost
> Which nightly gulls him with intelligence,
> As victors of my silence cannot boast;
> I was not sick of any fear from thence.

*Neither he - nor that friendly spook Homer who every night comes to him and fills his mind with rubbish – can boast they have silenced me. To be honest, neither writer nor ghost gave me the least apprehension.*

Shakespeare claims that his rival has been taught 'by spirits', just as Chapman had been by the spirit of Homer. He has also received 'aid' – patronage - from 'his com*peers* by night' - Strange, Northumberland and Carey. With the word 'sail/sale'

Shakespeare plays on Chapman's name: (chapman: pedlar OED). He does it more obviously in Sonnet 102:

> That love is merchandised, whose rich esteeming
> The owner's tongue doth publish everywhere

And even more in Sonnet 21:

> Let them say more that like of hearsay well
> I will not praise that purpose not to sell.

The references to Chapman are made even more blatantly in 'Love's Labour's Lost' itself. When Boyet utters his first line ('Now, Madame, summon up your dearest spirits') it was a clear reference to Chapman's known taste for seances. Boyet proceeds to heap tons of extravagant, sycophantic praise on the French Princess:

> Be now as prodigal of all dear grace
> As nature was in making graces dear
> When she did starve the general world beside,
> And prodigally gave them all to you.

*Be now as lavish with your loved gracefulness as nature was when she made gracefulness a rare and expensive commodity. She took all the world had and gave it to you.*

The Princess replies, coolly:

> Good Lord Boyet, my beauty though but mean
> Needs not the painted flourish of your praise.
> Beauty is bought by judgement of the eye
> Not uttered by base sale of chapmen's tongues.

In my Cambridge production of 'Love's Labour's Lost', an extravagantly baroque undergraduate called Gerald Chapman played the part of Boyet. The audience, who knew him, fell about with laughter at the mention of 'chapmen's tongues'. We had, unwittingly, 'summoned up' the original joke.

Shakespeare presents Chapman as the intriguing, narcissistic, sex-traitor Lord Boyet. Shakespeare had seen him flattering the Queen at first hand at Petworth. And, more alarmingly for Shakespeare, the young Harry himself. Berowne, in a passage of uncharacteristic cruelty, paints a grotesque picture of Boyet as one who -

> pecks up wit as pigeon's pease [seed]
> And utters it again when God doth please
> He is wit's pedlar and retails his wares
> At wakes and wassails, meetings, markets, fairs

Shakespeare goes on to add that this plagiarising effeminate, who has almost kissed his own hand away in courteous salutation, is even polite to bad dice at Backgammon. He sings the middle part between treble and bass because he is 'neither one thing nor the other'. The Ladies, however:

> call him, sweet;
> The stairs, as he treads on them, kiss his feet:
> This is the flower that smiles on everyone,
> To show his teeth as white as whales-bone:
> And consciences [people of good conscience]
>     that will not die in debt,
> Pay him the due of honey-tongued Boyet.

But Francis Meres (1565 - 1647) in 'Palladis Tamia: Wit's Treasury' (1598) describes Shakespeare himself as 'Honey-tongued' and his 'sonnets among his private friends' as 'sugared'.

It was eighteen years between Chapman's graduation from Oxford and the first publication of his 'The Hymn to Night' in 1594. Perhaps the 'old mocker' also worked as a 'generally nice person to have around' in a great household. And, like Shakespeare, had to flatter powerful women to survive. Berowne is also contemptuous of Boyet's sexual ambiguity, prophesying that 'a smock shall be [his] shroud'. Shakespeare seems to be disturbed by something stirring in himself.

But what he detests most in both Boyet and Chapman is their abuse of the English language. In Sonnet 21 he declares his difference to Chapman who 'stirred by a painted beauty to his verse' -

> heaven itself for ornament doth use,
> And every fair with his fair doth rehearse,
> Making a couplement of proud compare
> With Sun and Moon, with earth and sea's rich gems;
> With April's first-born flowers and all things rare
> That heaven's air in this huge rondure hems

*I don't want to write in the way my rival does. He gets his inspiration from the fake 'beauty' of a face plastered with make-up. He treats the heavens themselves as though they were a piece of junk jewellery. He extravagantly compares the beauty of the Queen with a jumbled mixture of sun and moon, gems from the earth and the sea, spring flowers and every unusual thing that the sky covers in this 'huge rondure' – his ridiculous name for the Earth.*

Elizabeth I comes to mind in the phrase 'painted beauty', especially as Chapman had praised her as Cynthia. Time and time again Shakespeare praises both natural beauty and a natural style of writing:

In Sonnet 82 he declares, in exasperation:

> yet when they have devised
> What strained touches Rhetoric can lend,
> Thou truly fair, wert truly sympathised
> In true plain words, by thy true telling friend;
> And their gross painting might be better used
> Where cheeks need blood; in thee it is abused.

*But when all those rival poets have finished trying to describe you in forced and unnatural language, you, who are truly beautiful both physically and morally, are better represented in honest to goodness language by me – who 'tells it like it is'. Their exaggerated cosmetic prose would be put to better use on cheeks that are drained of blood. With yourself as their subject, it is an abuse of language and an abuse of you.*

The cheeks that 'need blood' can have belonged to only one person.

Boyet, speaking of the King of Navarre's priapic response to the French Princess, obscures a simple, natural event by his complex, unnatural torture of the English tongue:

> Why all his behaviours did make their retire
> To the court of his eye, peeping thorough desire:
> His heart like an agate with your print impress'd,
> Proud with his form in his eye pride express'd...

And so on for another completely incomprehensible twelve lines. All Boyet means is that the King of Navarre has fallen in love. The Princess gives the right, dismissive response to this verbiage: 'Come to our pavilion: Boyet is dispos'd.' Later she asks Boyet to 'speak to be understood': but he is so locked into wordplay that he cannot express himself in a straightforward manner. In desperation the Princess cries: 'Avaunt perplexity!' But Shakespeare was the man who wrote this passage. Sometimes, in his Sonnets, he can be just as obscure as Boyet. Shakespeare is projecting all he cannot bear about himself into this other, shadow, 'Johannes fac totum.'

But Boyet has his qualities. Observant, he can often outwit his fellow men, dazed as they are by love. He is big enough to admit when he himself has been outclassed by the Ladies ('You are too hard for me') and is affectionate to Costard ('Good-night my good owl'). Shakespeare always gives full marks to people who are kind to Clowns. Berowne finally acknowledges that Boyet is 'allowed', like a jester, to speak his mind and congratulates him on one of his heckles during the playing of the Masque: 'Well said old mocker: I must needs be friend with thee'. This has echoes of Prospero's final realisation of his kinship with the monster Caliban:

This thing of darkness I acknowledge mine.

But Shakespeare had a much bigger fish to fry.

# CHAPTER 11.

# 'I THIRST FOR WALTER...'

Sir Walter Raleigh (1552-1618) spoke in a broad Devonshire accent all his life, was swarthy, often wore black clothes (he left them to his secretary/mathematician Thomas Hariot in his will) and was, according to Aubrey, 'damnable proud'. Because he came from a poor, if ancient, family (his father rented the house they lived in) Queen Elizabeth gave him the patent to export woolcloth in 1584.

According to Thomas Fuller, the Prebendary of Salisbury (1608-1661), writing in 'The History of the Worthies of England' (1662), the old schoolboy legend about Raleigh is true: he really did find 'the Queen walking, till, meeting with a plashy place, she seemed to scruple going theron'. Even though 'his clothes were then a considerable part of his estate' Raleigh 'cast and spread his new plush cloak on the ground; whence the Queen walked gently over...'

Because everyone thought the Spanish Armada would land in the South-West of England, Raleigh was given the strategically vital Lord Lieutenancy of Cornwall in 1585. Nonetheless, he was suspected of having 'a Spanish heart', receiving a Spanish pension and plotting for the Infanta of Spain to succeed Elizabeth. He wrote satirical poetry: but when, in his late 30's, he fell in love with Bess Throckmorton, one of Elizabeth's Ladies in Waiting, he started to write love-verse instead. Bess became pregnant, and the disgraced Raleigh was imprisoned in the Tower for the whole of August, 1592. His motto was 'Tam Marti quam Mercurio'. As much to Mars as Mercury.

The similarities with the play's Don Adriano de Armado are obvious, and noticed by scholars before. Described in the stage directions as a 'Braggart', Armado wears Spanish black to suit his 'sable-coloured melancholy'. He greets Holofernes with the broad West Country 'Chirrah' instead of 'Sirrah'*, is noble but poor, goes 'woolward for penance' and, Raleigh-like, literally worships the ground Jaquenetta stands on:

'I do affect the very ground, which is base, where her shoe, which is baser, guided by her foot, which is basest, doth tread.'

He threatens to write love-poetry to her – and in the final line of the play ('The words of Mercury are harsh after the songs of Apollo'), he echoes Raleigh's motto.

Don Armado was clearly based on Raleigh. And I believe events involving him in 1592 caused Shakespeare to hastily re-structure the conclusion of his play. At Christmas, 1591 Raleigh was a star at Court because of his brilliant account of the sinking of Sir Richard Grenville's 'Revenge'; but Bess Throckmorton was pregnant. The Queen jealously guarded her Ladies-in-Waiting and she became furious if any of her favourites fell in love with them. Raleigh, in his need, shamelessly courted Essex. Succumbing, as usual, to flattery, Essex stood as Godfather to Raleigh's baby son 'Damerei' on 10th April, 1592. On St. George's Day Essex even proposed to the Queen that Raleigh be made a Knight of the Garter.

In the play Don Armado admits to Moth he worships 'the wench' Jaquenetta, even though he has discovered her *in flagrante* with Costard. When he meets her, he blushes bright red and promises he will visit her at the Lodge:**

JAQUENETTA: That's hearby.

---

* A point made by M. C. Bradbrook in *The School of Night*, (1936)
** Another reference to Whitely Lodge, an appropriate place for the loose-living Jaquenetta to be imprisoned.

DON ARMADO: I know where it is situate.

JAQUENETTA: Lord how wise you are.

DON ARMADO: I will tell thee wonders.

JAQUENETTA: With that face?

DON ARMADO: I love thee.

JAQUENETTA: So I heard you say.

Jaquenetta makes her feelings for Don Armado plain. Yet at the end of the play we have the odd stage direction: 'Berowne steps forth', followed by Costard's warning to Don Armado that Jaquenetta 'is gone; she is two months on her way. Faith, unless you play the honest Trojan, the poor wench is cast away: she's quick, the child brags in her belly already: 'tis yours....'

How does Berowne know that Jaquenetta is pregnant - if that is meant by 'Berowne stands forth'? How does Costard know Don Armado is the father? How can Don Armado have impregnated her two months ago when we have seen her reject him the day before?

Shakespeare hurriedly changed the end of the play when he got news, via Essex and Southampton, of Bess Throckmorton's pregnancy. The Baptism was in early April: the play was performed on 14th May. By then Raleigh was waiting for a fair wind in Falmouth, desperate to fly England before Elizabeth discovered what everyone else knew.

So what was the original ending? Don Armado, hopelessly in love with his country wench, admits that 'Cupid's butt-shaft [an arrow to shoot at targets] is too hard for Hercules' club, and therefore too much odds for a Spaniard's rapier....Assist me some extemporal God of rhyme, for I am sure I shall turn sonnet'. We never get this poem: but there are two strange sonnets at the end of Shakespeare's own sequence, completely different in style and tone from the others, which mention Cupid's fire-brand. The first (Sonnet 153) tells how Cupid:

laid by his brand and fell asleep,
A maid of Dian's this advantage found,
And his love-kindling fire did quickly steep
In a cold valley-fountain of that ground;

*Cupid put down the fire-brand that he uses to inflame men's passions and fell asleep. One of the handmaidens of the chaste Goddess Diana took advantage of the situation: she seized the flaming brand and plunged it into a cold fountain.*

Which borrowed from this holy fire of love
A dateless lively heat still to endure,
And grew a seething bath which yet men prove
Against strange maladies a sovereign cure.

*But the sacred flame heated the water instead. The water, hot to this very day, is a bubbling bath which proves beneficial to men with venereal disease.*

But at my mistress' eye Love's brand new fired,
The boy for trial needs would touch my breast;
I sick withal, the help of bath desired,
And thither hied, a sad distempered guest,
But found no cure; the bath for my help lies
Where Cupid got new fire; my mistress' eyes.

*But my mistress's eyes sparked Cupid's brand into life: it caught fire again. Cupid, wanting to experiment on me, touched my breast with it. This caused me to fall love-sick. I needed 'the help of bath' and went there, an unlucky and diseased guest. But I found no cure: the only remedy for me lies in the same place where Cupid got new fire for his brand: my mistress's eyes.*

Sonnet 154 is very similar – and concludes:

but I, my Mistress' thrall,
Came there for cure, and this by that I prove:
Love's fire heats water, water cools not love.

*I, the slave of my mistress, came to the well for a cure: but I found that, though fire can heat water, water cannot cool down love.*

Are we to believe Shakespeare, after writing the most sublime sequence of poems in the language, presents himself as a fool who cannot distinguish between love-sickness and the clap? Scholars and playwrights, taking these end sonnets as literal autobiography, have confined Shakespeare to a syphilitic Stratford-upon-Avon retirement, nursed by his son-in-law Doctor, John Hall. The truth, I believe, is very different.

In October, 1582, Sir Thomas Heneage – later to be Mary Southampton's second husband - emerged from a clump of trees to confront Queen Elizabeth, holding a letter, a jewelled bodkin and a bucket. The letter, he explained, came from Sir Christopher Hatton, craving her love. The bodkin symbolised the dagger Hatton would use to kill himself if the Queen did not return his affection: the bucket symbolised 'Water/Walter'. The Queen was paying more attention to Sir Walter Raleigh than her own 'faithful sheep'. The Queen, replying that she would 'cherish Hatton in a meadow bounded by high banks so sure as no water nor floods should ever overthrow them', gave Heneage a dove to show 'there should be no more destruction by water'.

Queen Elizabeth would also often mock Raleigh's Devonshire accent by saying 'I thirst for Warter...'

The conclusion of Sonnet 154 ('Love's fire heats water, water cools not love') makes the same joke on the name of Sir Walter Raleigh. And the lines in Sonnet 153 -

> I, sick withal, the help of bath desired,
> And thither hied, a sad distempered guest

- refer to Raleigh's known fondness for taking curative waters at the town of Bath.*

---

* On 10th May, 1593 Raleigh wrote sadly to Cecil from Bath: 'I am the worse for the bath and not the better.'

These two sonnets are sketches for the poem Don Armado never delivers – not the intimate confessions of a diseased Shakespeare. Armado's labours of love, originally intended to be lost along with everyone else's, were to be lamented in a sonnet. Not being a native English speaker, he unwittingly implies that he has the clap. It is the same genre of joke as when Armado describes the afternoon as 'the posteriors of the day'. But Shakespeare always plays fair with his characters. He also shows Don Armado to be passionate, gracious and brave. He shouts down the Lords when they heckle him during his performance as Hector in the Masque, shaming them, in his halting English, into a respect for the dead:

'The sweet war-man is dead and rotten; sweet chucks, beat not the bones of the buried; when he breathed he was a man'.

Don Armado's pride is brought low when challenged to 'uncase' and fight with Costard. He has to admit that he is too poor to wear a shirt beneath his doublet. But, like the Lords in the play, he learns wisdom through humiliation. Sobered by the news of the death of the Princess's father, Don Armado, breathing 'free breath', determines to do right by Jaquenetta: he has 'seen the wrong through the little hole of discretion' and swears he 'will right' himself 'like a soldier.' But at the very moment he vows 'to hold the plough' for Jaquenetta's 'sweet love' for 'three year' he reminds us of a story told about him by Sir John Harington (1561-1612) in his 'Nugae Antiquae' (1769). When Raleigh saw Sherbourne Castle 'he cast such an eye upon it as Ahab did view Naboth's vineyard [that] suddenly over and over came his horse, that his very face, which was then thought a very good face, ploughed up the earth where he fell.'

Elizabeth, not knowing about Bess, had made Sherbourne a present to Raleigh at the beginning of 1592.

# CHAPTER 12.

## Merely players

Three of the group who read 'Love's Labour's Lost' at Titchfield were theatre directors, so, naturally enough, none of us could agree where the play had been originally staged. I favoured the knot-garden; its pathways and formal, complicated symmetry could mirror the convolutions of the language and the plot. But where would Berowne hide to overlook the Lords? And where would the audience sit? One director thought the front of 'Place House' would make a tremendous back-drop for the action; another favoured the Park where there would be trees to climb and bushes to hide behind. Gazing at the overgrown 'garden' on a subsequent visit to Titchfield, I began to fear that, four hundred years later, I would never know how the play was originally staged.

Then the penny dropped. Shakespeare wrote, 'All the world's a stage'. At Titchfield it was literally true. Titchfield itself was the set.

I believe the play followed the format of the Cowdray and Elvetham Progresses. Different parts of the play would be performed in different parts of the grounds. The audience, like Queen Elizabeth, would move to the appropriate spot for the action. When the Princess arrives at the doors of the Court, she arrives at the doors of 'Place House'. When she goes to hunt in the park, she goes to hunt in 'The Parke'. All the features of the estate could be exploited and celebrated. I began to understand why the time-scheme of the play is botched. Sometimes the action seems to take place over one day, sometimes two*. The production was originally staged over a couple of days.

---

* Boyet, when asked to produce the documents that prove the Princess's father has paid for Aquitaine, says: 'Tomorrow you shall have a sight of them.' Berowne gives Costard a sonnet to take to Rosaline in the park that afternoon: but the letter is actually delivered, during the hunt, the following day.

Shakespeare patched it up as a continuous play when he re-worked it for the theatre.

If the setting of the play was 'real', then why not the action itself? Why talk about deer-shooting when you can actually shoot deer? We know that two 'standings' were set up for Elizabeth at Titchfield in September, 1591. I believe they were used for the same purpose, eight months later, in the play itself. The parody of Elizabeth's Progress was complete.

●

Even the aristocrats in the audience for 'Love's Labour's Lost' would have been the same as those who attended the 1591 Progresses. And if the Earl of Essex was at Titchfield then his wife (Sidney's widow) and his sister, Penelope Rich (Sidney's 'Stella' in his sonnet sequence) would have been there too. Shakespeare uses the word 'rich' seven times in 'Love's Labour's Lost', twice in the context of wisdom ('wise and rich'/'rich wisdom'). He might have been employing the word, as Sidney did in his sonnet sequence, as a flattering reference to Penelope.

Shakespeare would have made sure all the people satirised in the play were in the audience. Florio was part of the Southampton household anyway: and if 'The School of Night' was invited, it would have been natural to include Chapman. And if George Carey was there, then so was the pamphleteer Thomas Nashe, his protégé, thought by many to be the original for the page-boy Moth. (Greene described Nashe as 'young juvenal': Don Armado describes Moth as 'tender juvenal'). Nashe was actually living with Carey on the Isle of Wight later that year.* Sir Walter Raleigh, as we know, was otherwise engaged at Falmouth.

---

* Katherine Duncan-Jones in *Ungentle Shakespeare*, (2001) suggests that it was really Nashe who wrote the 'upstart crow' attack: so it might have been Shakespeare's performance as Berowne he had in mind. The 'crow' could be a reference to Berowne's hiding in a tree.

There was one big difference between the audience for Elizabeth's Progresses and the audience for 'Love's Labour's Lost'. Jane, 1st Countess of Southampton, loved to invite the local people to watch the Christmas entertainments. As the play was produced within the context of a Whitsun Fair, the Toms, Dicks, Marians and Joans of the Southampton household - and the ordinary folk from the town, in their 'plain statute caps' - would have been a natural part of the audience.

In fact an essential part of the audience. When Holofernes, at the end of a scene with the most obscure word-play Shakespeare ever wrote (Act 5, Scene 1) says: 'Via, goodman Dull thou hast spoken no word all this while' and Dull replies: 'Nor understood none neither sir', Shakespeare needs the roar of their honest laughter. And when the King asks Costard if he has heard the proclamation that making love to a woman carries with it a year's imprisonment, they would have completely identified with Costard's reply: 'I do confess much of the hearing it, but little of the marking of it'.

Even in the presence of the King, Costard speaks his mind. He is suspicious of high-falutin' phrases and wants to know what they literally mean. ('Remuneration! O that's the Latin word for three farthings'). He is also the first to appreciate wit in others, like Moth, to whom he gives his 'remuneration' to buy ginger-bread. A natural gentleman, he leaps to the defence of Sir Nathaniel when the Curate forgets his words in the Masque: 'There, an't shall please you: a foolish mild man; an honest man, look you, and soon dashed! He is a marvellous good neighbour, faith, and a very good bowler, but for Alisander, - alas! You see how 'tis, - a little o'erparted.' In fact Costard, with his honesty, kindness, truth to himself and gentle common sense represents all that was best in the ordinary, uneducated Englishman. He is the 'Touchstone' of the play who, because he has no illusions about himself, can outwit the wittiest of the play's aristocrats. Shakespeare even gives him what was, before 'Mary Poppins', the longest word in the English language: 'honorificabilitudinitatibus'.

Costard also represents all that was best in Shakespeare. Hovering, as a poor relation, between the Lords and the commoners, Shakespeare knows that the unlettered life is close to 'barbarism': but he becomes concerned when language, straying too far from what it describes, takes on a perverse life of its own. He wants to extend the English language – that is why he devours Florio's new dictionary. But he does not want to destroy his own tongue with alien affectation. He seeks exactly the right word for the right occasion. He prefers women without make up and English without adornment. He wants to take the best that foreign countries have to offer in thought and sensibility: but he remains the strongest guardian of our own native wit.

●

So, to speculate: Harry Southampton, hero-worshipping his older friend, Robert Essex, and admiringly envious of his chivalric conduct in battle, invites him to a Whitsun joust at Titchfield. Mary Southampton, realising that Essex, with a growing tolerance to Catholics, is the coming man, perhaps the next King of England, adds to the fun of the Whitsun Fair by commissioning cousin Will to provide a new, romantic-satirical play. Let off lightly (financially, if not emotionally) by the Queen on her visit to Titchfield the previous year, Mary has the money to set up an extravagant, rival 'Male' Progress which feeds on the form of her father's Cowdray Progress, sends up its pretensions, and examines its implications. The event, lasting several days, includes the celebration of the Whitsun Service at St. Peter's, with the Bassanos, poached from Elizabeth, providing the

Pentecostal trumpet 'winds of God' as they had done for the Doge of Venice.

The service, which probably sneaks in a bit of forbidden Catholicism (a wooden dove hovering above the altar and rose petals falling from the rafters), includes the baptism of baby John Naylor, giving the whole congregation, dressed, like Essex in his habitual white,* the chance to re-new its baptismal vows. Perhaps Southampton acts as godfather, giving proof to Berowne's assertion at the beginning of the play that 'Every Godfather can give a name'. Black-faced, white-frocked Whitsun Morris Men, dancing in the churchyard the second the service is over, signal the start of the fair. The procession of grandees back to 'Place House' gives Essex, like Bolingbroke in 'Richard II', the chance to work the Titchfield crowd:

> Off goes his bonnet to an oyster-wench;
> A brace of draymen bid God speed him well,
> And had the tribute of his supple knee,
> With 'thanks my countrymen, my loving friends'.
>
> (Act 1, Scene 4)

The communicants break their fast with an *al fresco* green-goose Feast, washed down with the Vicar's Whitsun Ale, at a table even longer than the one at Cowdray. The Bassano trumpets signal the start of the Sunday afternoon tournament. Essex and Southampton, viewed by the noble Ladies from the 'standings', emerge in their orange armour from pavilions (later to be used as the 'tents' for the 'French Ladies' in the play) to offer mock impresas to a mock May-Queen and issue a joint challenge to any bold, young knights. Perhaps it was the sight of Southampton being hoisted onto his horse that Shakespeare remembers when he later writes:

---

* To show his allegiance to Queen Elizabeth.

106

I saw young Harry with his beaver [helmet] on,
His cushes [armour] on his thighs, gallantly arm'd,
Rise from the ground like feather'd Mercury,
And vaulted with such ease into his seat
As if an angel dropp'd down from the clouds
To turn and wind [round] a fiery Pegasus,
And witch the world with noble horsemanship.

(Henry IV Part 1, Act 4, Scene 1)

Sufficient lances broken, the triumphant young knights relaxed, what better than a diversion before supper?* Our instinct, when we read the play at Titchfield, was to eat after Berowne's declaration of his love for Rosaline. This first section lasts about an hour: it could well start at five o'clock and end 'about the sixth hour when [Don Armado writes] beasts most graze, birds best peck, and men sit down to that nourishment which is called supper'. The audience would be left with the cliff-hanging frisson of Berowne's confession of love for Rosaline, and, consequently, Shakespeare's for Emilia, as she sat, flattered and embarrassed, with her family in the 'delicate bower' provided for the band:

Well I will love, write, sigh, pray, sue, and groan
Some men must love my lady, and some Joan.

Mention of 'greasy Joan' would turn the thoughts of the audience, perhaps with some ambivalence, to their supper.

●

Who were the actors? Shakespeare, with 'Henry VI' running at the Rose, would have made contact with London players. With a tradition of amateur acting at Titchfield, my guess is that Southampton's friends and the local schoolboys played the more

---

* In 'Pericles' the knights are so eager to get on with 'revels' after the tilt they even dance in their armour.

shadowy Lords and Ladies and that Shakespeare and Mary hired a hard-core of male professionals to play the major parts. As well as a good, free meal, always welcome to actors, they could pitch their wits against the locals at the Fair. We can be sure that the Bassanos did some moon-lighting there as well.

The Whitsun Fair offers a solution to another puzzle in the play. Why can nobody count? Don Armado, as we would expect, cannot multiply one by three: but even the pedant Holofernes gets his sums wrong. Having cast five of the nine Worthies, he says 'I will play the other three myself'. This might be a slip by Shakespeare, notoriously sloppy about detail in his plays; but the theme is taken up again when Costard refers to 'the three Worthies'. Berowne questions this, and says there should be nine. Costard replies 'Every one pursents three'. 'And three times three is nine' counters Berowne. 'It were a pity you should get your living by reckoning, sir', replies Costard, enigmatically. Even the King reads out the names of five Worthies and says:

> And if these four Worthies in their first show thrive,
> These four will change habits and present the other
> five.

Berowne points out he has read the names of five, but the King says; 'You are deceived, 'tis not so.' What is going on?

Moth gives the answer when he says: 'How easy it is to put years to the word three, and study three years in two words, the dancing horse will tell you'. Holofernes also, when he condemns Berowne's poor verse-writing, refers to the author as a 'tired horse' who simply imitates his rider.

Malone, in his 1821 edition of 'Love's Labour's Lost', quotes Richard Farmer (1735-1797) who takes 'tired horse' to mean the 'attired' horse, 'the horse adorned with ribbons.' He even names it as Morocco, the amazing performing horse, owned by

Bankes, one of Essex's entourage, who could solve mathematical problems by pounding the earth with his hoof. He also quotes Sir Kenelm Digby (1603-1665) in 'A Treatise on Bodies' (1644) who describes how 'the horse would restore a glove to his true owner, after the master has whispered the man's name in his ear'. He would also beat out with his hoof 'the just number of pence in any piece of silver coin, newly showed him by his master' and even obey Bankes's command 'to discharge himself of his excrements.' Raleigh, in his 'A History of the World, Part Two' (1614), more philosophically observes that 'if Bankes had lived in former times, he would have shamed all the enchanters of the world: for whosoever was most famous among them, could never master or instruct any beast as he did his horse.' Bankes's snow-white horse, shod, it was rumoured, with pure silver, was, I believe, at Titchfield as part of the Fair. Shakespeare uses him as a moral lesson. Animals can add up, but idiot humans cannot.

Bankes and his wonderful horse had a horrifying end. Touring Europe, they survived accusations of Satanism by Capuchin monks in France: Bankes instructed Morocco to bow to anyone wearing a crucifix in his hat and then kiss the crucifix itself. In Rome, though, their luck ran out. Both were burnt at the stake by the Pope.*

---

* *The Dictionary of National Biography* doubts this story. But Malone quotes Dr. Isaac Reed (1742-1807) who quotes *Don Zara del Fogo* (1660) and Ben Jonson's *Epigrams 134:* 'Old Bankes the juggler, our Pythagoras,/Grave tutor to the learned horse. Both which,/Being beyond sea, burned for one witch.' Gervase Markham names the horse 'Curtal' in *Cavalry – or the English Horseman* (1607)

# CHAPTER 13.

# FAME

> At Christmas I no more desire a rose
> Than wish a snow in May's new-fangled shows;
> But like of each thing that in season grows.
> So you, to study now it is too late,
> Climb o'er the house to unlock the little gate.
> (Berowne, Act 1, Scene 1)

The first section of the play, I believe, was played outside the doors of 'Place House'. These doors still exist at the ruin, as does 'the little gate' within them whose 'threshold' Costard tripped over four hundred years ago when he breaks his shin. So 'Place House' and 'The Parke' become 'Navarre': Shakespeare honours both Southampton and Essex in one breath. Squeezing in yet another compliment, he names the King of Navarre 'Ferdinand'. Ferdinando, Lord Strange, with his interest in Shakespeare's writing, was most likely present at the play.

The opening lines would have provoked stirrings in the Essex/Sidney entourage:

> Let fame, that all hunt after in their lives
> Live registered upon our brazen tombs
> And then grace us in the disgrace of death
> When spite of cormorant devouring time
> Th' endeavour of this present breath may buy
> That honour which shall bate his scythe's keen edge,
> And make us heirs of all eternity

*All people hunt after celebrity in their lives: let's be content to achieve it in death – when it will give beauty to a humiliating process. We can defy Time, ravenously hungry for us, by the integrity of our current undertaking, which will dull the cutting edge of his scythe and make us famous forever.*

The motto painted on Sidney's portrait in The National Portrait Gallery is 'Caetara Fama' (The Rest is Fame). Southampton, as Burghley's student, had stated in a Latin essay barely three months before Sidney's death, that every man 'burns with boundless hope for fame'. Essex, at the premiere of the play, was probably wearing Sidney's sword, given to him as Sidney lay dying. But as the central question of the play revealed itself (how far can man master his natural inclinations by retreat, fasting and study?) every aristocrat and scholar in the audience would have leant forward with interest. Shakespeare is about to argue, as Falstaff was later to do, that fanaticism, of any kind, is an enemy to life. It can even kill you.

●

The year before, Swithin Wells, the Southampton family's loved old teacher and friend, had moved from Southampton House in London to his own dwelling nearby in Holborn. Topliffe (the arch priest-catcher who had a rack set up in his own home) raided the house in the middle of a Latin Mass. A scuffle on the stairs, between a lay communicant and Topliffe, led to a scene straight from a Graham Greene novel. The recusants swore they would give themselves up to certain death if they could continue to the end of the Mass in peace.

Wells was out at the time, but his wife was arrested and the keys to his house seized. Foolishly, Wells went to complain to Justice Young. He was immediately arrested himself. Though he had 'not been at the feast', quipped the Judge, he would 'taste of the sauce.' The Authorities, as usual, offered to free the Catholics if they would turn Protestant. The celebrant, a twenty-four year old priest called Edmund Genings (a former Protestant page-boy in a Catholic household whose conversion had been accompanied by shakings and visions and whose ordination at Reims had been fast-tracked through the previous year) was even offered a living. The Judge, though, found Genings' vehement defence of the Old Faith offensive. Put into a cage called 'Little Ease' where he could neither sit down nor stand up, Genings was starved till the day of his joint execution with Wells on the 10th December, 1591.

On Wells's way to the gallows, erected outside his home (pointedly a stone's throw from Southampton House) he saw an old acquaintance in the crowd. As Challoner says, 'he could not forget his wonted mirth but cried out, 'Farewell, dear friend; farewell all hawking, hunting and old pastimes; I am now going a better way". Genings angered Topliffe by giving a defiant speech to the crowd. The hangman got his revenge by 'scarce giving him liberty to say a Pater Noster' before turning him off the ladder. He cut the rope immediately so that Genings 'little or nothing stunned, stood on his feet, casting his eyes towards Heaven, till the Hangman tripped up his heels to make him fall on the block, on which he was to be quartered.' As his legs and arms were hacked off Genings screamed out in pain. Wells tried to comfort him by saying 'Alas, sweet soul, thy pain is great indeed but almost past; pray for me now, most holy saint, that mine may come'. When Genings 'was ripped open and his bowels cast into the fire...this blessed martyr (his heart being in the executioner's hands)' called on Saint Gregory, in Latin, to pray for him. Topliffe, on hearing this, 'swore a most wicked oath: 'Zounds! see his heart is in my hand, and yet Gregory is in his mouth. O! egregious Papist." Wells, displaying amazing sang-froid, asked Topliffe to get on with the business of hanging him: 'Are you not ashamed to suffer an old man to stand here in his shirt in the cold? I pray God make you, of a Paul, a Saul, of a persecutor, a Catholic professor'. He ended by forgiving Topliffe 'heartily'.

Caution, it hardly needs saying, is necessary with this account. Challoner was taking the story from Gening's brother, John, who was not at the execution. In fact, at the time, John was hostile both to Rome and Edmund. Tormented by guilt, he converted to Catholicism ten days later, became a Franciscan monk and published the life of his brother in 1614.

There is an intriguing note in the Privy Council minutes. They record how 'to make him [Genings] a scoff to the public' officers at his trial 'vested him (not now in his priestly garments in which they had before carried him through the streets) but in a ridiculous Fool's coat, which they had found in Mr. Wells' house'. What was a Fool's coat doing in Wells's house? Was Wells a jester, teaching Catholic truths through the Fool's cap and bells?

Like Campion, he had encouraged young Catholics to enter Douai and Reims to become missionary priests. They would have taken the same vows of chastity and obedience as the young Lords do at the beginning of 'Love's Labour's Lost'. They would have risen at five every morning, and fasted three days a week. Shakespeare had seen, at first hand, what happens to young men who embark on a heroic course of life. He might even have attended the execution of Wells and Genings, if only to report to the grieving Southamptons. He might even have been 'the old acquaintance' Wells joked with on the way to the scaffold.

The Wizard Earl, Northumberland, and Chapman's 'School of Night', by studying the stars, had also reversed the usual pattern of sleeping and waking. Berowne, addressing them directly in the audience as 'These earthly godfathers of heaven's lights', argues that there is a time and place for everything. It is not appropriate for young men, with youthful desires, to deny their very natures. The Whitsun Feast itself cries out against mortification of the flesh. For Berowne, true 'study' cannot come from books. It comes from a full engagement with life itself, revealed most fully in the eyes of a woman. 'Eyes' are mentioned thirty-two times in the play.

Shakespeare audaciously advances 'common sense' above heroism. It was the pursuit of the high, male ideals of chivalry that had led to Sidney's needless death. This same quest for glory was to lead to the execution of Essex and Raleigh. It was nearly to hang, draw and quarter Harry Southampton himself.

●

Berowne's reminder to the Lords that they have forgotten the visit of the French Princess and her ladies would have provoked wry smiles at Titchfield. Many in the audience would have spent months of preparation and hundreds, if not thousands, of pounds on the visit from Elizabeth a few months back. When the boy-actor playing the Princess arrives with her 'Ladies', probably side-saddle on horses from the Titchfield stable, he would inevitably mimic Elizabeth's arrival before the gates of 'Place House'.

The First Quarto, giving the game away by calling the Princess 'Queen' in the stage directions, has 'Shoot within' when the Princess goes to kill the deer. Some editors have changed this to 'Shout within'. This is wrong. Shakespeare was trying to suggest, in his stage version, the twang of the crossbow at Titchfield in 1592. The Bassanos probably played the same 'background music' to the slaughter they had used at Cowdray. Near the end of the play, when the Lords have been tricked, fooled and humiliated by the Ladies, Berowne says: 'Our states are forfeit: seek not to undo us.' Gervase Markham in 'The Gentleman's Academy' (1595) explains that 'Undoing' was a technical term in hunting. When the deer had been slain, it was the ritual duty of 'the best man of the company' to 'take the assay [penis] before the company then firm cut off the coddes'(a delicacy at table). Queen Elizabeth, as 'the best man of the company', had that duty to fulfil: a contemporary wood-cut shows her, knife in hand, approaching a supine stag. So the boy actor playing 'the Princess' could well have performed the same bloody ritual, in travesty, as the Queen did in September of the previous year.

Costume, wigs and make-up would have been another indication that Elizabeth was being guyed in the play. When, in 'The School of Night' passage, the King of Navarre says: 'And beauty's crest becomes the heavens well', I believe he is talking of the Princess's hair, flaming like a red sun in the 'heavens'. And when Berowne mentions her 'usurping hair', it refers to the rumour that Queen Elizabeth had lost all of hers. The boy playing the Princess would have worn a red wig.

There is another reference to Elizabeth when Berowne says to the Lords:

> O! If the streets were paved with thine eyes
> Her feet were much too dainty for such tread

To which Dumaine replies:

> O vile! Then, as she goes, what upward lies
> The street should see as she walk'd overhead

In the famous 'Ditchley' portrait, commissioned by her old tilting champion Lee, Queen Elizabeth spreads her frocks over the upturned eyes of Oxfordshire.

When the Princess of France says, 'But come, the bow', the Montague/Southampton family, having survived the Queen's Progress with their Priests and secret Masses 'undiscovered', would have cried out with relieved laughter. This was a reference to the highly ritualised moment in the Cowdray progress when a Nymph handed Elizabeth a cross-bow, quoted the family motto and Harry Southampton knelt.* The boy playing the Princess of France was probably handed the very bow Elizabeth had used at

---

* Shakespeare also refers to this motto in Sonnet 105: 'To one, of one, still such, and ever so'.

Cowdray. She had left it with Montague to hang as a trophy in Buck Hall.

Shakespeare then puts one of the most beautiful speeches he ever wrote into the mouth of the Princess:

> now mercy goes to kill,
> And shooting well is then accounted ill.
> Thus will I save my credit in the shoot:
> Not wounding, pity would not let me do't;
> If wounding, then it was to show my skill,
> That more for praise than purpose meant to kill

*My position is ambivalent: I claim to be merciful but I am about to kill. If I shoot my arrows well they will be seen to have done harm. I intend to protect my reputation by this ploy: if I do not hit the deer, I shall say that it was because I felt pity for it. If I do hit the deer, it was only to show my skill in shooting, not with the intention of killing the animal.*

> And out of question so it is sometimes,
> Glory grows guilty of detested crimes,
> When, for fame's sake, for praise, an outward part,
> We bend to that the working of the heart;
> As I for praise alone now seek to spill
> The poor dear's blood, that my heart means no ill.

*Certainly this quest for glory can lead on to atrocities when, in order to achieve fame, we ignore the workings of our heart. That is why I am in this predicament. In order to be praised, I must kill an animal that I pity.*

Shakespeare is trying to understand how Elizabeth, a woman of refined sensibilities and intelligence, tremendous self-knowledge, and finely tuned instinct can put her name to the death-warrant of people like Wells, a dear friend of the family she had visited three months before. He concludes it was her hunger for glory. She had, years before, admitted she wanted 'to do some act that would make her fame spread abroad in her lifetime, and, after, occasion memorial for ever'. She was even prepared to commit 'detested crimes' in order to achieve this immortality.

On her first entry, the Princess divines the King of Navarre's dilemma. If he keeps his oath, he cannot extend his hospitality. If he extends his hospitality, he cannot keep his oath. She introduces the great theme of the play: guilt, and how to deal with it. We must appreciate the solemnity of the vows the Lords take. From the moment the women arrive, the souls of the Lords are in jeopardy. They desperately seek a way to justify their sin. And the ladies exploit any weakness in the men. The Princess even mocks the poor Forester who, in answer to her question where she should hunt, says:

> Hereby upon the edge of yonder coppice;
> A stand where you may make the fairest shoot

The Princess wilfully misinterprets 'fairest' to be a compliment to her beauty rather than a description of the shoot. The Forester, honest enough to admit this was not his intention, is tortured mercilessly. The Princess compares him to a looking glass and pays him for telling the unkind truth. When he finally tries to praise her, she retorts:

> O heresy in fair, fit for these days!
> A giving hand, though foul, shall have fair praise

Queen Elizabeth was said, until the last moments of her life, to have banned all 'true' looking glasses from her presence.

The Princess is not alone in this attitude to men: later in the play Rosaline openly admits:

> That same Berowne I'll torture ere I go.
> O! that I knew he were but in by the week [besotted]

> How I would make him fawn, and beg, and seek,
> And wait the season, and observe the times,
> And spend his prodigal wits in bootless rimes,
> And shape his service wholly to my hests
> And make him proud to make me proud that jests!
> So Pair-Taunt like would I o'ersway his state
> That he should be my fool, and I his fate.

The sadism here is as disturbing as the undoing of the deer. When Rosaline says she will make Berowne 'proud' she means 'erect'. She will derive pleasure through Berowne's sexual frustration in enforced servitude. Shakespeare is honest enough to admit that some women delight in confusing the instincts of men. 'Pair-Taunt' is to have a winning hand at cards: Rosaline is quite prepared to make a game of a man's destiny.

The women do not have it all their own way. Costard arrives and the Princess intends to mock him like the simple Forester. He asks who is 'the head lady?'. The Princess replies: 'Thou shalt know her, fellow, by the rest that have no heads.' Costard tries again: 'Which is the greatest lady, the highest?'. The Princess springs her own trap: 'The thickest and the tallest'. To which Costard replies:

> The thickest and the tallest! It is so; truth is truth.
> And your waist, mistress, were as slender as my wit,
> One o' these maid's girdles for your waist should be fit.
> Are not you the chief woman? You are the thickest here.

The Princess changes the subject.

My experience in directing comedy is the more 'real' the pain the actors are in, the funnier the situation is to the audience. That is why the scene in which the Lords spy on one another is such a masterpiece. Each Lord comes into the Park to read his love-poem to his mistress. But the verse is full of desperate, special pleading as each Lord tries to justify his perjury. And each, uncharitably, hopes the other Lords will break their vows so the guilt can be shared.

Berowne watches the Lords, 'All hid, all hid; an old infant play', with ironic detachment from 'above'. The King has asked 'sweet leaves' to 'shade' the 'folly' of his sonnet. He is himself 'closely shrouded' in a bush. What more natural place to play this scene than in 'The Parke' itself? What more natural place for Berowne to hide, Puck-like, than in a tree? Berowne's cry of 'God amend us, God amend!' harks back to the 'old infant' Corpus Chrisiti plays enacted in those very grounds, once the property of the Abbey. The fun is that each Lord steps forward to denounce in others the sin he is most guilty of himself. At the height of his hypocrisy, Berowne quotes Christ:

> You found his mote; the King your mote did see;
> But I a beam do find in each of three

But Costard and Jaquenetta, the play's 'true folks' because true to themselves and their own natures, arrive with Berowne's love-sonnet to Rosaline. Incriminating himself by tearing it to pieces, Berowne is forced to exclaim:

> Guilty, my lord, guilty! I confess, I confess

The Lords, like Essex at Rouen, defend the superior beauty of their respective mistresses, but then the King calls a halt:

> KING
> But what of this? Are we not all in love?
>
> BEROWNE
> O! Nothing so sure; and thereby all forsworn.
>
> KING
> Then leave this chat; and good Berowne, now prove
> Our loving lawful, and our faith not torn.

**DUMAINE**

Ay, marry, there; some flattery for this evil.

**LONGAVILLE**

O! some authority how to proceed;
Some tricks, some quillets [subtleties] how to
cheat the devil.

**DUMAINE**

Some salve for perjury.

Here we have the dilemma for Catholics. How do you deal with guilt, in a non-Catholic world? In the old days, the Lords would have confessed to a priest. Now they have to forge their own redemption. That is the glory, and shortcoming, of the world Shakespeare inherited and the dramatic world he created.

Berowne argues brilliantly, like the lawyer Shakespeare might once have been, that there is no need for remorse: the vow that the men have taken, 'to fast, to study and to see no women' was 'flat treason 'gainst the kingly state youth'. Young men must not deny their stomachs food. Though they might have neglected their books, they have not neglected their studies. How would they have discovered true knowledge without a woman's beauty?

But Love, first learned in a lady's eyes,
Lives not alone immured in the brain,
But with the motion of all elements,
Courses as swift as thought in every power,
And gives to every power a double power,
Above their functions and their offices.
It adds a precious seeing to the eye;
A lover's eyes will gaze an eagle blind;
A lover's ear will hear the lowest sound,
When the suspicious head of theft is stopp'd:
Love's feeling is more soft and sensible

Than are the tender horns of cockled snails;
Love's tongue proves dainty Bacchus gross in taste.
For valour is not Love a Hercules,
Still climbing trees in the Hesperides?
Subtle as Sphinx; as sweet and musical
As bright Apollo's lute, strung with his hair;
And when Love speaks, the voice of all the Gods
Make heaven drowsy with the harmony.

*But love taught by the eyes of a woman does not live locked up in
the brain; it enhances all the senses as well. A lover will see further
than an eagle, hear tiny sounds even a nervous burglar will miss,
become more sensitive than the delicate horns of a snail. He loses his
taste for wine, but gains the valour of Hercules, the sophistication of
the Sphinx and the brilliant lyricism of the God Apollo. A lover,
speaking with the voice of all the Gods, will even enrapture the
Heavens.*

No poet should think of writing before 'his ink' has been
'tempered with love's sighs': then he can entrance savage men
and humble tyrants. Women's eyes, burning with the
Promethean fire of inspiration, are the books, the studies and the
colleges which 'show, contain and nourish all the world'.

What audacity Shakespeare has shown with this speech. The
ungowned son of a glover, the 'upstart crow', stands in a field in
Titchfield and tells his noble relatives and the most learned
scholars in Elizabethan England that they are all wasting their
time. Was there anywhere else in the world this could have
happened?

There was one scholar, present at least in spirit, who would
have relished what Berowne has to say. With only a slight adjust-
ment to his sonnet in 'Astrophil and Stella', Sir Philip Sidney
could have added his voice to Shakespeare's: 'Fools, look in your
hearts and write!'. But Shakespeare, in this scene, has surprises

still. Berowne, having convinced the Lords to woo and win the Ladies, suddenly has doubts. Can any good come of a venture that starts by breaking a vow?

> Sow'd cockle reaped no corn;
> And justice always whirls in equal measure:
> Light wenches may prove plagues to men forsworn;
> If so, our copper buys no better treasure.

*If you have sown darnel weed, you can't expect a crop of corn – and justice works both ways. Flippant women may prove deadly to men who have broken their vows: if so, it is no better than our base natures deserve.*

Shakespeare, forever seeking the truth, is prepared to undermine totally one of the greatest passages he ever wrote. As a married man about to seduce Emilia, he was very aware of the vow he himself was breaking: and in the way the Lords try to justify their perjury with their poems, Shakespeare suddenly realises he is trying to justify his own by writing the play itself.

# CHAPTER 14.

# JACK HATH NOT JILL

The Lords decide to woo the Ladies dressed as Russians. 'Enter Black-moores with musicke, the Boy with a speach, and the rest of the Lordes disguysed' runs the stage-direction from the First Quarto. Why do Blackamoors enter? What have Blackamoors to do with Russia? Scholars have made heroic attempts to find literary precedents: but the answer is obvious. When the directions say Blackamoors enter 'with musicke' it means that they are playing instruments. Shakespeare's musicians were the dark-skinned Bassano family. If he puts them onstage, they have to be 'Black-moores'.

Why didn't the Lords themselves disguise as 'Black-moores' as well? This would have mimicked the Whitsun black-face Morris dancers and poked gentle fun at Rosaline/Emilia and her dark-skinned family. It would also have continued the black/white imagery of the play, first introduced by Don Armado when he writes about 'that most obscene and preposterous event [Costard's 'seduction' of Jaquenetta] that draweth from my snow-white pen the ebon-coloured ink'. The word 'black' is used eleven times in the play, the word 'white' twelve. The imagery comes into sharpest focus with Rosaline's 'black' hand concealed by her white glove. Perhaps, in the original Titchfield production, the Lords did black up, or use black masks. We only have the 'augmented' script for the winter production of the play before Elizabeth six years later. The Russian interlude could well be one of these 'augmentations'. 'Frozen Muscovites', with snow on their boots, would be perfect for the Queen at Christmas-time.*

---

* A Christmas entertainment, sometimes attributed to Francis Bacon, 'Gesta Grayorum', was performed at the Inns of Court in the Christmas period of 1594/5. 'Russians' appear in the piece to enlist the help of the English to fight the Tartars. One of them, like Berowne, is described as 'sea-sick'. Perhaps Shakespeare, always 'a snapper-up of unconsidered trifles', lifted the Russian idea for the Queen's entertainment from 'Gesta Grayorum'.

When the Lords return as themselves, to the mocks of the women who reveal they knew the Lords' plan from the start, there is an extraordinary exchange. The King asks the Princess, as he has earlier asked Berowne, to provide some 'fair excuse' for the men's behaviour. The Princess replies; 'The fairest is confession'. But she does not mean the King should see a priest. She means he should confess to her.

> PRINCESS
> Were not you here but even now disguised?
>
> KING
> Madam, I was.
>
> PRINCESS
> And were you well advised? [In your right mind]
>
> KING
> I was, fair madam.
>
> PRINCESS
>        When you then were here,
> What did you whisper in your Lady's ear?
>
> KING
> That more than all the world I did respect her.
>
> PRINCESS
> When she shall challenge this, you will reject her.
>
> KING
> Upon mine honour no!
>
> PRINCESS
>        Peace, peace, forbear:
> Your oath once broke, you force not [value not] to
>     forswear.
>
> KING
> Despise me, when I break this oath of mine.

PRINCESS
I will; and therefore keep it.

The King is reduced to mumbling monosyllables, like a naughty boy in front of a strict headmistress, or an errant courtier in front of Queen Elizabeth. In a world without Catholic Priests, someone has to be Confessor. If that someone is your lover, Shakespeare asks, can the love possibly survive? Can the King grovel, humiliated and silenced by the Princess, and then win her heart? The Princess reveals that the women all changed favours, so the Lords wooed the wrong Ladies. They have broken their vows yet again…

●

'The Masque of the Nine Worthies' which follows is a parody of the Progress entertainments Elizabeth endured the previous year. Don Armado implores the Princess 'so much expense of thy royal sweet breath as will utter a brace of words.' The Princess is being asked to perform in the Pageant, just as Elizabeth was obliged to take speaking parts at Cowdray and Elvetham.

'The ship is under sail – and here she comes amain' says the King. The Worthies probably arrive in a mock-galleon on a pageant wagon, satirising the water sports in Lord Hertford's lake. Costard, with unconscious ribaldry, announces to the audience he represents Pompey 'surnamed the Big' and explains that:

> travelling along this coast I here am come
>   by chance
> And lay my arms before the legs of this sweet lass of
>   France

And so he presents his shield to the Princess of France as all 'the Noblemen and Gentlemen of the Shire' had done at

Cowdray. But Pompey, like Hercules, was never one of the Nine Worthies. Hercules is included as a compliment to Navarre. To whom is Pompey a compliment?

The people of Portsmouth. Portsmouth, and the Portsmouth Football Team, are known to this day as 'Pompey'. No one seems to know when the nick-name started, but a despairing hand-out from the Portsmouth Tourist Information Centre suggests an origin in Elizabethan times. It cites two quotations from 'Antony and Cleopatra': 'Pompey is strong at sea' and 'Sextus Pompeius hath given the dare to Caesar, and commands the Empire of the sea'. One theory is that 'Pompey' was an imitation of a drunken sailor trying to say 'Portsmouth Point'. Certainly when Costard says: 'I Pompey am', he falls over.

In 1592 Costard could literally have travelled 'by chance' along the coast from Portsmouth (ten miles away) and up the River Meon to Titchfield. Many visitors would have found themselves in the area 'by chance' when Queen Elizabeth called.

And when Costard has finished his performance as Pompey, he prompts the Princess: 'If your ladyship would say, 'Thanks Pompey', I had done'. 'Thanks Pompey' was the 'brace of words' her 'royal sweet breath' was meant to utter.

●

Act Five Scene Two of 'Love's Labour's Lost' is one of the longest scenes in Shakespeare. Probably in its original form it was broken up into two sections, with a supper break, so that the Masque could be performed in the growing dusk. Queen Elizabeth had witnessed a torch-lit procession of sugar works at Elvetham; and three years later, at the Accession Tilts, Essex was to employ the same formula of joust, supper break and play. There are also textual indications that darkness is falling. Boyet says: 'A light for Monsieur Judas! It grows dark, he may stumble'. And when, in a brilliant coup, Marcade arrives to announce the death of the Princess's father, Berowne says: 'Worthies away! The scene begins to cloud'.

Shakespeare turns a light comedy into a Morality Play. He tests the protestations of eternal love against death itself. And the love is found to be wanting.

The Princess admits that the news has robbed her of her easy eloquence. When the King tries awkwardly to both comfort and woo her at the same time he simply doubles her grief. Berowne tries 'honest plain words': but his arguments (and this could be Shakespeare's fault) sound too much like the legalistic pleading he has employed elsewhere:

> we to ourselves prove false,
> By being once false for ever to be true
> To those that make us both – fair ladies, you:
> And even that falsehood, in itself a sin,
> Thus purifies itself and turns to grace

*We have been false to ourselves – but having done that once, we can now be true forever to those who make us both true and false – beautiful ladies, yourselves. And even that lie, though admittedly a sin, by this action redeems itself and becomes acceptable to Heaven.*

The Princess says she took the courtship as a merry game, 'as bombast and as lining to the time' and though the King asks her 'at the latest minute of the hour' to return his love, it is too soon for the Princess. Having broken his vow, the King must show his love by deeds rather than words. He must spend a year in a 'forlorn and naked hermitage/Remote from all the pleasures of the world'. Berowne asks for some similar task to be imposed, but is dismayed by Rosaline's demand that he 'jest a twelve-month in a hospital':

> To move wild laughter in the throat of death?
> It cannot be – it is impossible;
> Mirth cannot move a soul in agony.

Rosaline explains that this is the way to 'choke' Berowne's 'gibing spirit' and makes a pact with him. If sick people are amused by his wit, then she will accept that characteristic in him: but if he fails, then he must 'throw away that spirit' and Rosaline will welcome Berowne's 'reformation'. He agrees to Rosaline's conditions, but adds:

> Our wooing doth not end like an old play:
> Jack hath not Jill. These ladies' courtesy
> Might well have made a sport a comedy

The King reminds him that the period of penance will only last for a year and a day. But Berowne, leaping from the confines of the theatre back into life itself, declares: 'That's too long for a play'.

The women have destroyed the self-respect of the Lords; now they demand the men change their very natures. Where would Berowne be without his 'gibing spirit'? That is what makes him who he is. At a time when a powerful Queen was also trying to get her subjects to change their very souls, where does this leave a man? How can he properly love a woman who takes upon herself the 'reformation' of his spirit?

I believe Shakespeare set out to write a happy comedy that ended, 'like an old play', with the marriage bed. I believe he intended to use the play, like the initial Sonnets, to persuade Southampton to marry. But as he worked on the material, in the shadow of Wells's execution, he found a resolution impossible. Death, in the Southampton family, had loomed too large.

Shakespeare has unbalanced his play, but he has opened the way to a far more complex relationship with young Harry.

# CHAPTER 15.

# AMOROUS STARS

What did Mary Southampton think of the play she had commissioned? To answer this question we must return to the Elvetham Progress. As part of Queen Elizabeth's entertainment on the third day at Lord Hertford's estate, three musicians, 'disguised in ancient country attire' sang 'The Plowman's Song' at her casement window:

> In the merry month of May,
> In a morn, by break of day,
> Forth I walked by the wood side
> Where as May was in his pride...

This is very similar in tone to Dumaine's love-poem which begins:

> On a day, alack the day!
> Love whose month is ever May
> Spied a blossom passing fair
> Playing in the wanton air...

Both poems, the first attributed to Nicholas Breton (c.1555-1626) and the second to Shakespeare, were published a few pages away from each other in 'England's Helicon', (1600). Shakespeare, influenced by Breton, might have read the printed account of the Elvetham Progress. But it is much more likely that he was actually present at the entertainment as part of the Southampton entourage. He 'replied' to it – a custom amongst Elizabethans – in 'Love's Labour's Lost'.

But Shakespeare was not only present at Elvetham. I believe he wrote the strange encounter between Elizabeth and the 'real' Fairy Queen who appeared at the bottom of her garden.

Lord Hertford's text runs: 'Her Majesty was no sooner ready, and at her gallery window looking into the garden, but there began three cornets to play certain fantastic dances, at the measure whereof the Fairy Queen came into the garden, dancing with her maids about her. She brought with her a garland, made in the form of an imperial crown; [which] within the sight of Her Majesty she fixed upon a silver staff, and, sticking the staff into the ground, spake as followeth:

The Speech of the Fairy Queen to Her Majesty.

> I that abide in places underground,
> Aureola, the Queen of Fairy land,
> That every night in rings of painted flowers
> Turn round, and carol out Elisa's name:
> Hearing that Nereus and the Sylvan Gods
> Have lately welcomed your Imperial Grace,
> Opened the earth with this enchanting wand,
> To do my duty to your Majesty,
> And humbly to salute you with this chaplet,
> Given me by Auberon, the Fairy King.
> Bright shining Phoebe [Elizabeth], that in human
>     shape
> Hid'st heaven's perfection, vouchsafe t'accept it:
> And I Aureola, belov'd in heaven,
> (For amorous stars fall nightly in my lap)
> Will cause that heavens enlarge they golden days
> And cut them short, that envy at thy praise.

After this speech, the Fairy Queen and her maids danced about the garland singing a song of six parts, with the music of an exquisite consort....

> Elisa is the fairest Queen
> That ever trod upon this green.
> Elisa's eyes are blessed stars

Inducing peace, subduing wars.
Elisa's hand is crystal bright,
Her words are balm, her looks are light...'

It is dangerous, as we have seen, to attribute writing to Shakespeare: but I believe the Fairy Queen's sublime line -

For amorous stars fall nightly in my lap

- anticipates Oberon's:

And certain stars shot madly from their spheres

And the heavy four beats per line of the Fairies' song look forward to Oberon's last speech in 'A Midsummer Night's Dream':

Now until the break of day,
Through the house each fairy stray...

But the implication of the speech, that there is a power in the Heavens far greater than any human monarch, which needs to be acknowledged for a reign and a life to prosper, is very Shakespearean indeed. The ambiguity of the notion that Elizabeth was 'hiding' the perfection of the Heavens in mortal shape is matched by the ambiguity of the chaplet dangling from the silver staff. Was it accepted or not? Elizabeth demanded three encores and 'called for divers Lords and Ladies to behold it': but she went straight back to Richmond to inaugurate a Catholic witch-hunt. Aureola, I contend, was an early sketch for Titania – and a challenge from a Catholic, however light and oblique, to Elizabeth's spiritual supremacy.

There is a local tradition at Copped Hall in Epping Forest that 'A Midsummer Night's Dream' was first performed there to celebrate the marriage of Sir Thomas Heneage (1533-1595) to Mary Southampton in 1594. Mary heard cousin Will's lyrics (she might even have been one of the 'divers Lords and Ladies' invited to Elizabeth's chambers) and, delighted by 'Love's

Labour's Lost', commissioned Shakespeare to expand the Fairy Queen idea into a full-length play - one in which 'Jack' finally does gets 'Jill'.

'A Midsummer Night's Dream', like the Progresses and like 'Love's Labour's Lost', was, I believe, performed over several days. The moonlit forest scene was played in genuine moonlight in the forest at the foot of the hill that leads up to Copped Hall, between 'after supper and bed-time'. The Duke's oak, where Bottom and the Mechanicals meet for their night rehearsal, was a real oak – as were the hawthorn-bush that acts as their tiring-house and the bank that Hermia lies on. When Oberon orders Puck to 'overcast the night' and cover 'the starry welkin' with 'drooping fog as black as Acheron', the effect was achieved by lighting fires of wet grass. The immortals, emerging from the darkness of the wood, had the true ambivalence of Tudor Fairy Folk. The lovers, when they sleep 'on the dank and dirty ground', were left by the audience and 'discovered' next morning as though they had been there all night.

Before Duke Theseus wakes them he says to Hippolyta:

> My love shall hear the music of my hounds.
> Uncouple in the Western valley; let them go;
> Dispatch, I say, and find the forester

And later adds:

> My hounds are bred out of the Spartan kind,
> So flewed [large-chapped] so sanded [sand-coloured]
>     and their heads are hung
> With ears that sweep away the morning dew;
> Crook-knee'd and dewlapp'd like Thessalian bulls
> Slow in pursuit, but match'd in mouth like bells,
> Each under each: a cry more tuneable
> Was never holla'd to, nor cheered with horn,

In Crete, in Sparta, nor in Thessaly.
(Act 4, Scene 1)

Why does Shakespeare hold up the action of the play with a totally irrelevant speech about Theseus's hounds?

The answer is they were Sir Thomas Heneage's hounds and Shakespeare is paying the Bridegroom a gentle compliment. Sir Thomas himself, famed for his 'elegancy of life and pleasantness of speech', in a private performance could well have played Theseus with Mary Southampton as his mature Hippolyta. At a signal his hounds were probably uncoupled in the western valley down from Copped Hall. The same effect could also have been created in 'Love's Labour's Lost'. When the Princess asks at the beginning of Act 4 -

Was that the king who spurred his horse so hard
Against the steep-uprising of the hill?

- the scene probably began with a tremendous display of riding up the steep 'high eastern' Titchfield Hill.

Sir Thomas and Mary were married on 2nd May, 1594. Heneage was in his sixties and Mary was 44, but age was not the only difference. Heneage was a Protestant and as Vice-Chamberlain attended Anti-Papist Privy Council meetings, including one held during the Cowdray Progress in 1591. A Church marriage service would have embarrassed both sets of friends and family: so they most likely settled for a private ceremony, probably at the Savoy, Heneage's London home. Mary commissioned Shakespeare to write a Midsummer celebration, much as 'Love's Labour's Lost' had been a Whitsun one, to honour Sir Thomas's house and grounds - now her own house and grounds. When, in the first scene, Theseus says:

but o, methinks, how slow
This old moon wanes! She lingers my desires,

> Like to a step-dame or a dowager
> Long withering out a young man's revenue

Shakespeare was sending up Mary's stringent control of Southampton's finances.* Harry was to come of age later in the year – a celebration at Titchfield his mother pointedly did not attend. And when Theseus says -

> Hippolyta, I woo'd thee with my sword
> And won thy love doing thee injuries

- Heneage is apologising to Mary for the persecution of her Catholic family and friends.

One of the central themes of the play – how far young people should follow the wishes of their parents in the choice of a partner, and how far the dictates of their heart - was being acted out in the Southampton family itself. Shakespeare argues tolerance for Harry as Theseus finally overrules Egeus's demand that Hermia should wed Demetrius.

The major discord in the play comes from the fight between Oberon and Titania for possession of the 'little changeling boy'. Shakespeare was obliquely referring to the fight between Mary Southampton and her first husband, the 2nd Earl, over the possession of little Harry. He shows, in the disturbance of nature, the spiritual repercussions on all concerned of such a bitter conflict. He uses the magic of his verse to heal this old family wound. Titania and Oberon are finally reconciled: the old marriage has to be symbolically closed before the new one can begin.

This discord in the fairy world had an echo in reality. The summer of 1594 was appalling. Forman, Emilia Bassano's astrologer, tells us that 'June and July were very wet and wonderful cold like winter, that the 10th day of July many did sit

---

* A point Anthony Holden also makes in *William Shakespeare: his Life and Work* (1999)

by the fire it was so cold; and so it was in May and June...there were many great floods this summer.' All of which Titania describes in the play itself:

> The ox hath therefore stretched his yoke in vain,
> The ploughman lost his sweat, and the green corn
> Hath rotted ere his youth attain'd a beard;
> The fold stands empty in the drowned field,
> And crows are fatted with murrion [diseased] flock.
> The nine-men's morris is fill'd up with mud...
>
> (Act 2, Scene 1)

As the play was intended to show off the grounds of Mary's new house and the night scenes to be played under the moon, there was no point in producing it indoors. Everybody just waited for the weather to improve. According to John Stow (c. 1525 - 1605), the tailor and antiquarian, the weather rallied in August of 1594: that is when the play was finally performed.

Confirmation comes from 'Willobie his Avisa' - a strange work which purports to be a poem left in the study of an Oxford undergraduate, Henry Willobie, who 'being desirous to see the fashions of other countries' has 'departed voluntarily to Her Majesty's service'. Hadrian Dorrell, a friend entrusted with Willobie's key, claims to have found the poem and published it, without the author's permission, in 1594. The poem is a satire on men who unsuccessfully attempt to seduce 'Avisa', an inn-keeper's chaste wife. Two of the suitors are H.W. (a young man called 'Harry' who employs Florio's Italian tags) and W.S., an 'old player' who, having been rebuffed by 'Avisa', maliciously encourages his young friend to woo her and so suffer the same humiliation. H.W. – called 'Italo-Hispalensis' in reference to his Catholicism, and Spanish Catholicism at that - is obviously meant to suggest Henry Wriothesley and W.S., Shakespeare. Shakespeare and his poem 'The Rape of Lucrece' are mentioned directly in the text.

The situation is complicated by the fact that there really was an Oxford student called Henry Willobie, very distantly related to Shakespeare. But whoever wrote the satire had inside information. Material from the Sonnets, not to be printed for another fifteen years, is alluded to in the poem: and 'The Rape of Lucrece' was entered at Stationer's Halls in May of 1594, a mere four months before 'Willobie his Avisa'. But the fascinating link with 'A Midsummer Night's Dream' is H.W.'s description of Avisa's garden, 'With pleasant flowers lately decked/With cowslips and with eglantine,/When woeful woodbine lies reject'.* In Act 2, Scene 1 Puck mentions cowslips twice: 'The cowslips tall her pensioners be' and 'I must go seek some dew-drops here,/And hang a pearl in every cowslip's ear'. But, more significantly, Oberon in the same scene rhymes 'woodbine' with 'eglantine':

> I know a bank where the wild thyme blows,
> Where oxlips and the and the nodding violet grows
> Quite over-canopied with luscious woodbine,
> With sweet musk-roses, and with eglantine.

Whoever wrote 'Willobie his Avisa' had seen the first production of 'A Midsummer Night's Dream' (the play was not published till 1600). As 'Willobie his Avisa' was entered in the Stationer's Register on 3rd September, 1594, that must be the latest date for the production of the play. The August hypothesis fits perfectly.

It also fits with a topical allusion. James VI's son, Prince Henry, was born in Scotland on 19th February, 1594. A great Baptismal Feast was planned for the 30th August, later that year, with a theatrical coup. In the middle of the feast, a chariot would appear, drawn by a lion. It is unlikely that there were any lions in Scotland in 1594: but we do know there were lions in the

---

* As Eric Sams points out.

Tower of London. James VI and I was later to disgust his son Prince Henry by throwing beagles to them. So James most likely sent to London for a lion. As many ambitious Elizabethans made it their business to know everything James did, the lion quest would be the talk of the town.

However, 'A True Reportarie', registered on 24th October, 1594, apologises for the fact that at Prince Henry's Baptismal Feast the chariot that 'should have been drawn in by a lion' was drawn in by a blackamoor because the lion's 'presence might have brought some fear to the nearest, or that the sights of the lights and the torches might have commoved his tameness'.

What this really means is that James could not find a lion. Shakespeare satirises this excuse (which would have been known by James-watchers way before the publication of 'A True Reportarie') in 'A Midsummer Night's Dream'. Bottom offers to play the part of the lion in the Mechanicals' play but Quince reacts in horror: 'And you should do it too terribly, you would fright the Duchess and the ladies, that they would shriek: and that were enough to hang us all.'

●

There is a fairy called Moth in 'A Midsummer Night's Dream' just as there is the page-boy called Moth in 'Love's Labour's Lost'. The word 'Jew' is also used as a compliment. Flute, playing the part of Thisbe, says:

> Most radiant Pyramus, most lily-white of hue,
> Of colour like the red rose on triumphant briar,
> Most brisky juvenal, and eke most lovely Jew
> (Act 3, Scene 1)

In 1594 Anthony Bassano, who probably played Moth in 'Love's Labour's Lost', would have been 14, so, like Flute, would have 'a beard coming'. If Anthony Bassano played Flute, he could also have played the fairy Moth (the Mechanicals often double with the Fairies in production). Shakespeare, perhaps at Mary's request, was writing in a part for the Jewish Bassano boy – and alluding to his triumph as Moth two years earlier.

●

Shakespeare had a problem. Heneage, a former favourite of Elizabeth, was still a close friend of the Queen. She had given Copped Hall to her 'Sanguine' in 1564, so he was duty bound to invite her to the play*. A compliment was needed for Elizabeth, always touchy about weddings. But Mary Southampton's friends and family, probably half the audience, were predominantly Catholic. Copped Hall also had associations with Mary Tudor: she had been imprisoned there and stubbornly refused to give up celebrating the Catholic Mass. A compliment to the Queen, whose spies had raided the homes of Catholics and whose hangmen had butchered their priests, friends and relatives, could be deeply offensive. Shakespeare, treading on egg-shells, again exploits the ambiguity of English.

Theseus warns Hermia that if she disobeys her father she must either 'die the death' or 'abjure forever the society of men'. He questions her whether she -

> can endure the livery of a nun,
> For aye to be in shady cloister mew'd, [cooped up]
> To live a barren sister all your life,
> Chanting faint hymns to the cold, fruitless moon.
> Thrice blessed they that master so their blood
> To undergo such maiden pilgrimage;
> But earthlier happy is the rose distill'd

---

* We will probably never know if Elizabeth attended. All Privy Council minutes between 1594-6 have been lost. But in the Public Record Office there is an account of a payment to Shakespeare for 'two comedies or interludes' before the Queen at Christmas, 1594. (E351/542). So perhaps she had seen the play earlier in the year — and liked it.

Than that which, withering on the virgin thorn,
Grows, lives, and dies, in single blessedness.

(Act 1, Scene 1)

Elizabeth, forever associated with the moon, could take this as praise of her heroic, other-worldly celibacy. She would hear the words 'blessed', 'master', 'pilgrimage' and 'virgin'. But her enemies would hear 'barren', 'faint', 'cold', 'fruitless', 'withering', 'thorn' and, above all, 'earthlier happy'.

Oberon, obviously toadying to Elizabeth, describes how Cupid, aiming one of his arrows at 'a fair vestal, throned by the west', had his 'fiery shaft/Quench'd in the chaste beams of the wat'ry moon':

And the imperial votress passed on,
In maiden meditation, fancy-free

But before he says this, Oberon asks Puck if he remembers that –

once I sat upon a promontory,
And heard a mermaid on a dolphin's back
Uttering such dulcet and harmonious breath
That the rude sea grew civil at her song
And certain stars shot madly from their spheres
To hear the sea-maid's music

(Act 2, Scene 1)

Bishop Warburton thought that 'the mermaid stands for some eminent personage of [Elizabeth's] time' and that 'the allegorical covering, in which there is a mixture of satire and panegyric, will lead us to conclude that this person was one of whom it had been inconvenient for the author to speak openly, either in praise or dispraise.' He concludes that the mermaid stands for Mary, Queen of Scots, beheaded seven years earlier, and the dolphin 'represents her marriage with the dauphin of

France, son of Henry II'. 'The rude sea', Warburton believes, is 'Scotland...which rose up in arms against the regent while she was in France'. The 'certain stars' which 'shot madly from their spheres' are 'the Earls of Northumberland and Westmorland, who fell in her [Mary's] quarrel; and principally the great Duke of Norfolk, whose projected marriage with her was attended with such fatal consequences'.

Shakespeare, I believe, was aiming nearer home - at Mary's first husband, the 2nd Earl, and her dead father, Lord Montague. Catholics would interpret 'madly' as 'passionately', Protestants, including the Queen, as 'insane'. The Mermaid also symbolised prostitution – as a contemporary political cartoon depicting Mary, Queen of Scots reveals. Shakespeare had performed the balancing act of all time.

But Shakespeare lets Catholicism have the last word. Oberon, lit by moonlight streaming in through the casement windows of the Great Hall, the 'dead and drowsy fire' in the grate and the tapers twinkling in the Fairies' hands, solemnly declares:

> To the best bride-bed will we,
> Which by us shall blessed be.
> And the issue there create
> Ever shall be fortunate
> So shall all the couples three
> Ever true in loving be...
>
> With this field-dew consecrate,
> Every fairy take his gait;
> And each several chamber bless
> Through this palace with sweet peace;
> And ever shall in safety rest
> And the owner of it blest.

(Act 5, Scene 2)

Fr. Bowden has pointed out that this reads 'almost like a paraphrase' of the Catholic 'Benedicto Thalami' (Blessing on the Bed-chamber): 'Bless, O Lord, this bed. May all who dwell in it remain in Thy peace, abide in Thy will, grow to old age, and be multiplied to the length of days, and attain at last to the Kingdom of Heaven. Through Christ our Lord'.

Shakespeare, paradoxically, was using English paganism to reinforce Catholic ideas. The fairy world, with its colour, passion and ritual, was nearer to the Old Religion than Elizabeth's stark, candle-starved Protestantism. He points out to Elizabeth, as he had done on the Elvetham Progress, that there is another Fairy Queen, centuries older than herself, who, though forced to live 'underground', more nearly represents the Catholic Queen of Heaven.

The woman who played the Fairy Queen in the private garden at Elvetham was, I believe, the dark-skinned beauty, Emilia Bassano, a true Black Madonna, favourite of the Queen and mistress to Lord Hunsdon, a canter away at Farnham on the eve of her performance. Shakespeare created the Fairy Queen for Emilia – then fell in love with his creation.

He declared that love in 'Love's Labour's Lost'.

# CHAPTER 16

# LOVE SICKNESS

Circumstances favoured Shakespeare's love-suit – clues to which are littered through the play. Boyet, intimating to the Princess that the King of Navarre loves her, says 'Navarre is infected'. Berowne, finding himself infatuated with Rosaline, exclaims:

> Go to; it is a plague
> That Cupid will impose for my neglect
> Of his almighty dreadful little might.

And, discovering he is so addicted to word-play he cannot even woo his love in plain English, admits he has -

> a trick
> Of the old rage: bear with me I am sick;
> I'll leave it by degrees.

*I still have a habit from my old illness: forgive me, I'm not well. I'll get better bit by bit.*

He continues -

> Soft! Let us see:
> Write 'Lord have mercy on us' on those three;
> They are infected, in their hearts it lies;
> They have the plague, and caught it of your eyes:

*What to do next? Write a plague warning – 'Lord have mercy on us' - on those three other Lords as you would do on an infected house. The Lords are heart-sick. They are plague-victims – and they caught the disease from your eyes.*

> These lords are visited; you are not free,
> For the Lord's tokens on you do I see

*They are infected: but you are not free from disease yourselves. I can see plague marks on you – 'the Lord's tokens' [both pock-marks and the gifts the Lords have given the Ladies].*

The Plague is used in 'Love's Labour's Lost' as a metaphor for love: but by the Summer of 1592 London was suffering from the worst real Plague, and drought, for a quarter of a century. The Thames dried up so completely you could ride across it on a horse. The run of 'Henry VI Part One' finished on 19th June. Shakespeare, like most authors, would have attended the last performance. We know for certain, from the letter about 'the bare ruined choirs' of Beaulieu signed by Southampton, that the two men were in London on 27th June. Even with a London hit on his hands, Shakespeare was still acting as the loyal factotum. After June the theatres were closed, first because of riot, then by mid-summer, because of the epidemic. Apart from two short winter seasons, the theatres were effectively 'dark' for twenty months. Deaths in Southwark, south of the river, were even higher than in the City itself.

What could be more natural for the Southamptons (who were never fond of London anyway), Shakespeare and Emilia to stay in Titchfield? Even Hunsdon, in his own interest, would have allowed his mistress the relative safety of the country. She had been useful to the Countess of Kent in her youth. She could perform the same service for Mary Southampton. And with nothing much else to do in Titchfield, she could become Shakespeare's mistress.

Despite her lies and her promiscuity, there is no doubt she gave Shakespeare a great deal of pleasure. He confesses in Sonnet 138:

> When my love swears that she is made of truth
> I do believe her, though I know she lies
> That she might think me some untutored youth,
> Unlearned in the world's false subtleties.

*When my lover gives me her word that she has been truthful to me, I believe her – even though I know her to be lying. The point of this is to make her think I am naïve – and consequently younger than I am.* \*

> Thus vainly thinking that she thinks me young
> Although she knows my days are past the best,
> Simply I credit her false-speaking tongue,
> On both sides thus is simple truth suppressed:

*So, with a hopelessly deluded belief she thinks I'm young – though she knows full well I've gone to seed - with a stupid frankness I believe her lies. That way we keep 'truth' - at once straightforward and dim - hidden from us both.*

Emilia's lies, along with her favours, serve to comfort and flatter Shakespeare. He plays upon the 'double-meaning' of 'to lie':

> Therefore I lie with her, and she with me,
> And in our faults, by lies, we flattered be.

There are times, in love, when it is indeed folly to be wise.

Often there is a bawdy ease in his relationship with Emilia. In Sonnet 151 he describes, with disarming honesty, his 'flesh' rising at 'her name' and pointing her out. And even when, in Sonnet 129, he acknowledges the humiliating agonies of lust ('perjur'd, murd'rous, bloody, full of blame/Savage, extreme, rude, cruel, not to trust') he still admits that no man knows how 'to shun the heaven that leads men to this hell'.

But we can see in 'Love's Labour's Lost' that Shakespeare, if not on the turn, was beginning to have doubts about heterosexual relationships. He started out as a completely 'straight', not to say rampant, Catholic country boy: but his

---

\* In Sonnet 73 he writes:
    When yellow leaves, or none, or few do hang
    Upon those boughs, which shake against the cold
Shakespeare was going bald early.

association with the Southamptons opened his life to every sort of possibility. He had been completely genuine in his desire that Southampton should marry. At this point he had children himself and was to become very close to his older daughter, Susanna. Even in one of his darkest plays, 'King Lear', Cordelia's love for her wilful old father brings him close to redemption.

Suddenly, in Sonnet 18, something extraordinary happens:

Shall I compare thee to a Summer's day?
Thou art more lovely and more temperate:
Rough winds do shake the darling buds of May,
And Summer's lease hath all too short a date:

*I'm not going to compare you to a summer's day. You are more beautiful than that – and less extreme. Even in May, rude winds shake the delicate buds: summer only has a short lease on the property it is renting.*

Sometime too hot the eye of heaven shines,
And often is his gold complexion dimm'd;
And every fair from fair sometime declines,
By chance, or nature's changing course, untrimm'd:

*Some days the sun is too hot: more often the sky is overcast. Everything that is beautiful at sometime or other will lose its beauty, either by what happens to it by chance, or by the natural process of ageing.*

But thy eternal Summer shall not fade,
Nor lose possession of that fair thou ow'st,
Nor shall death brag thou wand'rst in his shade
When in eternal lines to time thou grow'st:

*But the summer you possess will last for ever; nor will the beauty you possess ever be snatched from you. Death himself will not be able to boast that you walk in his shadow. In fact, my description of you will make you even more famous and beautiful as time goes by.*

So long as men can breathe, or eyes can see,
So long lives this, and this gives life to thee.

*As long as people recite poetry, or read it, this poem will last. And, by lasting, give you immortality.*

Shakespeare has fallen in love with Harry.

I believe there is a two year gap between Sonnet 17 – the last Birthday Sonnet – and Sonnet 18. The language is quite different – and so was Shakespeare. He had written 'Venus and Adonis'. This was printed for the public in 1593, but written, I believe, after Harry Southampton's seventeenth birthday in October, 1590 and before the production of 'Love's Labour's Lost'. It has a rather stiff, formal dedication to the 3rd Earl:

'I know not how I shall offend in dedicating my unpolished lines to your Lordship, nor how the world will censure me for choosing so strong a prop to support so weak a burden...'

At the same time John Clapham, Burghley's secretary, was writing 'Narcissus', another poem on an Ovidian theme – also dedicated to Southampton and printed in 1591. It deals with the legend of Narcissus, a young man initially fed on 'the warm milk of error' (Catholicism) who mounts a steed called 'Lust' and dies in the spring of 'Self Love', infatuated with his own reflection. Shakespeare's poem is about the Goddess Venus's unrequited love for the beautiful young Adonis who refuses her embraces and dies in a boar hunt. Although the poem is dedicated to Southampton, Mary Southampton still controlled his finances and Burghley was his guardian. I believe they commissioned Shakespeare, as Burghley commissioned his secretary, to continue to put pressure on Harry to marry and warn him of the deadly consequences of pursuing a homosexual life.

Shakespeare makes reference to Mary Southampton in 'Venus and Adonis' as he had done in his sonnets:

Art thou a woman's son and canst not feel
What 'tis to love, how want of love tormenteth?
Oh had thy mother borne so hard a mind,
She had not brought forth thee, but died unkind
(ll. 201-204)

In the first 17 Sonnets, by urging heterosexual love-making on Harry, Shakespeare had unwittingly involved himself with Southampton in an intimate way. Sonnet 4 uses money as symbol of semen to make disparaging reference to the boy's masturbation:

Unthrifty loveliness why dost thou spend
Upon thyself thy beauty's legacy?

And Sonnet 9 continues this criticism by mixing sex with death – a favourite theme of the Tudors:

No love toward others in that bosom sits
That on himself such murd'rous shame commits.

This inevitable convolution is the central theme of 'Venus and Adonis'. Shakespeare sets out to fulfil the terms of his commission – to celebrate the joys of heterosexual love. He shows how Adonis's stallion bolts off in heat with a jennet and praises this natural passion to shame Harry's coldness. But Shakespeare was an instinctive dramatist. He can see every side to a situation – and empathises with everybody's point of view. By pursuing the beautiful Adonis, Venus becomes a surrogate man, dismounting Adonis and hurling him to the ground like a rugby player. She even wishes that Adonis 'wert as I am, and I a man' – so Shakespeare, in his unconscious, is beginning to imagine what sex with Southampton himself would be like.

Adonis can also see through Venus. She claims to be Nature's agent of procreation, but lending 'embracements to every stranger', she really only wants to exercise her 'sweating lust'. The 'wayward boy' though 'unripe', has a notion of how true love, possibly gay love, contrasts with Venus's boiling blood:

> Love comforteth like sunshine after rain
> But Lust's effect is tempest after sun;
> Love's gentle spring doth always fresh remain,
> Lust's winter comes ere summer half be done;
> Love surfeits not, Lust like a glutton dies;
> Love is all truth, Lust full of forged lies.
>
> (ll. 799-804)

So Adonis's wish 'to hunt the boar with certain of his friends' is packed with implication. Mary and Burghley wanted a moral tale: Shakespeare, as an artist, packs the death of Adonis with rich, erotic ambivalence. Even at Cowdray, Elizabeth's slaying of 'the hart' was a pun on slaying 'the heart' of her favourites. Venus goes so far as to say that the boar which gored Adonis was actually trying to kiss him:

> 'Tis true, 'tis true, thus was Adonis slain:
> He ran upon the boar with his sharp spear,
> Who did not whet his teeth at him again,
> But by a kiss thought to persuade him there;
> And nuzzling in his flank, the loving swine
> Sheath'd unaware the tusk in his soft groin.
>
> (ll. 1,111-1,116)

Is the image of the sprawled Adonis, exposing 'the wide wound that the boar had trench'd/In his soft flank,' blood covering every 'grass, herb, leaf or weed' and nature seeming to bleed with him, an image of gory death – or of sublime, homosexual orgasm? Perhaps Shakespeare himself, at this stage, was not sure.

But he was sure, when he met Emilia Bassano at Cowdray, he

fancied her like mad and made an ostentatious bid for her at the end of the first half of 'Love's Labour's Lost'. Harry Southampton, emotionally starved, and as Shakespeare says in Sonnet 84, 'fond on praise', was used to being the centre of Shakespeare's attention. Wanting Shakespeare all for himself, he starts to wave Chapman's rival love-poems under his nose.

Harry had been under immense pressure all his young life. His mother, who wrote 'he never was kind to me' (which really means 'I never was kind to him'), had used him as a pawn. His father had encouraged his misogyny. Even his grandfather, with his propensity for golden-haired college theatricals and women-torture, could well have passed on to his grandson mixed feelings about the opposite sex.

Burghley had tried to 'convert' him in every way. At Cambridge he would have met more than his fair share of Nicholas Udalls. And on the Cowdray Progress his family had tried to sacrifice him, as a boy-lover, to the ageing Queen. Beautiful, and potentially rich, he was a prey to all. And all were a prey to him. Philip Stringer, a witness of the Queen's visit to Oxford in the autumn of 1592, describes him in a Latin poem as 'a Prince of a distinguished race...no youth there present was more beautiful or more brilliant in the learned arts than this young prince of Hampshire, although his face was yet scarcely adorned by a tender down'.*

I believe that Southampton, in the boredom of the plague-summer, set about seducing Shakespeare, as he was to seduce many others in the course of his life. Sonnet 20 is Shakespeare's confused response to these approaches. He prefers Harry's relative straightforwardness to Emilia's capriciousness:

---

* This sounds very like Venus's description of Adonis: 'The tender spring upon thy tempting lip/Shows thee unripe' (ll.127-8.)

> A Woman's face with nature's own hand painted
> Hast thou, the Master Mistress of my passion;
> A woman's gentle heart but not acquainted
> With shifting change, as is false women's fashion

*You are both my master and my mistress: your face, created by Nature itself, has the beauty of a woman's. You have the sensibility of a woman, but not Emilia's fickleness.*

But Shakespeare cannot bring himself, at this stage, to admit there is any physical basis to his love for the boy. He politely rejects Harry's advances:

> And for a woman wert thou first created,
> Till nature as she wrought thee fell a-doting,
> And by addition me of thee defeated,
> By adding one thing to my purpose nothing

*Nature first intended to make you a woman: but as she created you, she fell hopelessly in love with you – and gave you an extra something that means I cannot possess you, something of no use to me.*

> But since she pricked thee out for women's pleasure,
> Mine be thy love and thy love's use their treasure.

*So since she gave you a 'prick' to please women, give me your spiritual love, them your physical.*

Emilia, eyes everywhere, saw what was going on. Far more interested in the young Lord than the rapidly ageing writer, she manufactures a quarrel with Shakespeare in the hope he will send young Harry to sort it out. Shakespeare, with what Ben Jonson (1572-1637) calls 'an open and free nature', obliges. In Sonnet 134 he even apologises to his friend who came 'debtor for [his] sake' for this 'unkind abuse'.

If there was any 'abuse' it certainly was not Shakepeare's. Like Olivia in 'Twelfth Night', Emilia woos the go-between. Southampton becomes one of the 'many noblemen' who, in

Forman's notes, gave her 'great gifts' and 'made much of' her. Her father had died when she was seven, not bothering to legitimise her by marrying her mother. Emilia needed the love of men to make up for this loss. But she also resented them.

In Sonnet 133 Shakespeare lambastes Emilia for her betrayal:

> Beshrew that heart that makes my heart to groan
> For that deep wound it gives my friend and me;
> Is't not enough to torture me alone,
> But slave to slavery my sweet'st friend must be?

*Damn you for making me suffer. You give a 'deep wound' both to my friend and myself: and when I say 'deep wound' I'm referring to your genitals as well as the effect it has on both of us. Wasn't it enough to torment just me? Do you have to trap my friend as well?*

In Sonnet 41 Shakespeare even reproaches Southampton directly:

> Ay me, but yet thou might'st my seat forbear,
> And chide thy beauty, and thy straying youth,
> Who lead thee in their riot even there

But in Sonnet 40, he begins to wise up. He realises that Southampton, who did not care for women, was sleeping with Emilia simply to spite him:

> But yet be blamed, if thou thyself deceivest
> By wilful taste of what thyself refusest.

This emotional manipulation exactly parallels that of the aristocratic seducer in 'A Lover's Complaint' – Shakespeare's tail-piece to the Sonnets – whose 'passion' was 'an act of craft' and whose technique was to 'exclaim against the thing he sought' and 'preach pure maid' while 'burning with heart-wished luxury'*.

---

* Like Harry Southampton, he had 'browny locks' which hung 'in crooked curls' and 'sexes both enchanted'.

In Sonnet 42 Shakespeare begins to admit to himself that the loss of Emilia is not so important to him as the loss of his intimacy with Southampton:

> That thou hast her it is not all my grief,
> And yet it may be said I lov'd her dearly;
> That she hath thee is of my wailing chief,
> A loss in love that touches me more nearly

*That you've won Emilia from me isn't the chief cause of my pain, even though I really did love her. It's the fact that she's got you that kills me.*

In the anguished jealousy of Sonnet 144, when Shakespeare imagines Emilia and Harry in bed together, he finally acknowledges whose body he prefers:

> To win me soon to hell my female evil
> Tempteth my better angel from my side,
> And would corrupt my saint to be a devil,
> Wooing his purity with her foul pride;

*In order to damn me, this she-devil tries to tempt my boy-angel away from me. She wants to corrupt my saint into becoming a demon like her and uses all her debased sexuality to achieve her object.*

> And whether that my angel be turn'd fiend
> Suspect I may, yet not directly tell;
> But being both from me both to each friend,
> I guess one angel in another's hell.

*But, though I suspect it, I cannot know for certain whether this Satanic transformation has taken place. But as they are both away from me, and both 'friends', I suspect his angelic penis is in her hellish, diseased, pudenda.*

Lord Strange's company, to avoid the plague in London, starts a tour of the provinces on 13th July, 1592. Shakespeare, feeling desperately rejected by Harry and Emilia, and guilty about breaking his marriage vows to his wife, joins it to get away from everything and everybody. The low-born Helena, in 'All's Well That Ends Well', wins the 'bright particular star', the aristocratic young Bertram, by the potency of her healing. Shakespeare sets about winning Southampton back by the potency of his verse.

Southampton makes love to Emilia in July and August. She becomes pregnant and is married to the 'minstrel' Alphonse Lanier 'for colour' on 10th October, 1592. Like the 'Lover's Complaint' seducer, Harry is growing his plants 'in others' orchards'.

Two years later Emilia attends the first performance of 'A Midsummer Night's Dream' with the rest of the Bassano family, looking daggers at Southampton and Shakespeare, and parading her two year old son.

His name was Henry.

●

Years later we find a connection between Southampton and Lanier. In 1604 Bancroft, the Bishop of London, informs Sir Robert Cecil that 'Captain Alphonso Lanier, the late Queen's and now his Majesty's servant, mine old fellow and loving friend, has obtained a suit of his Highness for the weighing of hay and straw about London. He was put in hope of your favour by the Earl of Southampton'. Southampton was trying to provide for his bastard son.

Emilia was later to run a school, and, as a Christian convert from Judaism, publish her own collection of poems, 'Salve Deus Rex Iudeaeorum' (Hail God, King of the Jews) in 1611. In this, a disguised begging letter, she praises named, chaste noble-women, attacks fickle men and dedicates her poems to 'all the virtuous Ladies and Gentlewomen of this kingdom'. The author of 'Willobie his Avisa' dedicates the book to 'all the constant Ladies and Gentlewomen that fear God'. Emilia describes men as 'vipers' who 'deface the wombs wherein they were bred'. The Willobie author describes men as having 'tongues' which 'are tipped with poison'.

I suspect Emilia wrote this satire, with all its insider knowledge, to get her revenge on Shakespeare and Southampton, to try to demean their friendship and to keep Southampton under financial control by the implied threat of further revelations.

She re-invents herself as 'Avisa' – a down-market Queen Elizabeth, signing herself with the Queen's 'Semper Eadem' – a woman who never, ever succumbed to the seductive blandishments of men. She describes Harry Southampton as a cry-baby 'trickling tears, like rivers' who should 'marry with some honest wife'. She is 'loathe to see [his] blobbered face/And loathe to hear a young man cry'. She describes him as 'a headlong youth' and at one point even 'a boy'. She even hints at gay goings on amongst the aristocracy:

> Our English soil, to Sodom's sink
> Excessive sins transformed of late,
> Of foul deceit the loathsome link
> Hath worn all faith clean out of date,
> The greatest sins 'mongst greatest sort
> Are counted now but for a sport.

She also has a dig at Lord Hunsdon as well. He appears as an old, closet Catholic Nobleman, trying to seduce Avisa with his money:

> Here's forty angels to begin;
> A little pledge of great good-will,
> To buy thee lace, to buy a pin;
> I will be careful of thee still:

If youth be quailed, if I be old,
I can supply that with my gold.

Hunsdon, as we have seen, gave Emilia £40 a year to be his mistress. The last edition of 'Willobie his Avisa' was in 1635: Emilia died in 1645, at 76, still, presumably, collecting what royalties she could. At least she out-lived her lovers.

●

Shakespeare, on tour with Lord Strange's company, began to turn his private experiences into public theatre. 'The Two Gentleman of Verona' deals with the love of two men for the same woman. Valentine gives up his claim to Silvia to preserve his friendship with Proteus. Audiences and critics alike, not knowing the gay sub-text, have found this turn of events ludicrous.

Shakespeare might well have written 'The Taming of the Shrew' as a response to the more basic, heterosexual needs of the audience, uninterested in love between Lords but very keen to see a proud, beautiful young woman dominated by a swaggering man. Shakespeare might even have identified with Katharina...

●

As so often happens, he and Southampton grew closer by being parted. The love developed, by sonnet correspondence, into a full-blown affair on his return with Lord Strange's company to the town of Southampton the following year. But a gay relationship could lead to the block the same way a Latin Mass could.*

In 1533, Henry VIII had introduced a statute forbidding

---

* Southampton and Shakespeare probably attended secret Masses in the private chapel of 'Place House'. Catholic worship could well have been the illicit background to their illicit love. In Sonnet 31 Shakespeare talks of his 'dear religious love' for dead friends and in Sonnet 52 of 'feasts so solemn and so rare,/Since seldom coming in the long year set'. In 'As You Like It', Rosalind says of Orlando: 'And his kissing is as full of sanctity as the touch of holy bread'. (Act 3, Scene 4)

'buggery' on 'pain of death and loss of goods'. Mary Tudor had repealed this act in 1553: but Elizabeth revived it in 1562 claiming 'divers evil-disposed persons have been more bold to commit the said most horrible and detestable vice of buggery aforesaid, to the high displeasure of Almighty God'. So certain was Elizabeth that she was enacting God's will, that along with other statutes out-lawing fortune-tellers and gypsies, she made this one 'perpetual'.

So Shakespeare, though he made sure to seal his sonnets with wax, had to write to Southampton in code. In Sonnet 20, for example, the seventh line reads (in the original printing):

A man in hew all *Hews* in his controwling
*Some-one with a man's countenance – who makes every other countenance blush at his beauty.*

Shakespeare, with *'Hews'* is secretly playing on the initials of his lover, Henry Wriothesley, Earl (of) Southampton. And he describes their love-making in a roundabout way:

Sweet love, renew thy force; be it not said
Thy edge should blunter be than appetite
(Sonnet 56)

But sometimes, as in the conclusion to Sonnet 61, the love between Shakespeare and Southampton not only dares to speak its name; it yells it from the rooftops:

It is my love that keeps mine eye awake,
Mine own true love that doth my rest defeat,
To play the watchman ever for thy sake.
For thee watch I, whilst thou dost wake elsewhere,
From me far off, with others all too near.

*It is my own love for you that keeps my eyes open, my own faithful love that keeps me awake at night. It makes me play the part of a night watchman. I watch you, wide awake, somewhere else: far away from me – but far too close to others in bed with you.*

Shakespeare's constant fear is that he loves Southampton more than Southampton, a serial seducer, loves him. The plural 'others' in the sonnet may be literal. When James VI came to the English throne he employed twelve Scottish youths as 'gentlemen of the bedchamber'.

An anonymous informer, years later, sent a letter to Cecil about a Captain called Pearse Edmones 'a corporal general of the horse in Ireland under the Earl of Southampton. He ate and drank at his table and lay in his tent. The Earl of Southampton gave him a horse, which Edmones refused a 100 marks for him. The Earl of Southampton would cole and huge [fondle and hug] him in his arms and play wantonly with him.'

Shakespeare would have been the first to recognise this behaviour in Southampton: the ruthless 'lascivious boy' Bertram in 'All's Well That Ends Well' with 'his arched brows, his hawking eye, his curls' is a heterosexual version of Harry. Bertram and Southampton were both Wards of Court, both are eager to prove themselves in the wars and both end up as Captains of Horse. It is difficult to see why Helena in the play is so besotted with this 'unbaked and doughy youth' who rejects and abuses her so completely. Shakespeare, at the cost of the play's credibility, is projecting onto Helena his infatuation with Southampton.

The scene when Helena confesses her love for Bertram to his Catholic Countess mother can be read as 'transmuted' autobiography, the way reality is re-shaped by the alchemy of dreams:

COUNTESS
Do you love my son?

HELENA
Your pardon, noble mistress!

COUNTESS
Love you my son?

HELENA
Do not you love him madam?

COUNTESS
Go not about; my love hath in't a bond [legitimacy]
Whereof the world takes note. Come, come, disclose
The state of your affection, for your passions
Have to the full appeach'd. [confessed against you]

HELENA
                    Then I confess
Here on my knee, before high heaven and you,
That before you, and next unto high heaven,
I love your son...

(Act 1, Scene 3)

I believe the 'adopted' Shakespeare, prompted like Helena,
opened his heart to Mary Southampton. She, like the Countess,
remembering her own 'folly', her unfulfilled passion for 'a
common person' in her youth, gave the relationship her blessing.
She thought Shakespeare was a good, loving influence on her
wayward, distant son. She was certainly fond enough of
Shakespeare to ask him to write a play for her wedding. And in
the same year Shakespeare was confident enough of her favour
to express his adoration for her son in print. In his Dedication to
Southampton of the 'untutored lines' of 'The Rape of Lucrece',
Shakespeare declares: 'The love I dedicate to your Lordship is
without end....What I have done is yours, what I have to do is
yours, being part in all I have devoted yours...'

Sometimes, though, Shakespeare, like Helena, invites
Southampton to treat him like a door-mat. In Sonnet 57 he
actually casts himself as Southampton's 'sad slave' who, far from

esenting Harry's absence with other lovers, thinks that he has no rights at all on the boy's time. Love is so 'true a fool' that Shakespeare can find 'no ill' even in Southampton's promiscuous excesses.

But, unlike Helena, Shakespeare is prepared to speak his mind to Southampton. In his greatest and most complex Sonnet 94, using 'hurt' in its Chaucerean sense of arousing others sexually, he gives him a tremendous warning:

> They that have power to hurt, and will do none,
> That do not do the thing they most do show,
> Who, moving others, are themselves as stone,
> Unmoved, cold, and to temptation slow:

*Those who have the ability to arouse love in others and refrain from doing so; who do not engage in making love, no matter how much their cod-pieces show off their manliness; who, although they excite others, remain stone-like themselves, unroused, cool and reluctant to succumb to temptation -*

> They rightly do inherit heaven's graces,
> And husband nature's riches from expense;
> They are the lords and owners of their faces,
> Others, but stewards of their excellence.

*These people rightly inherit the grace of heaven, rather than the favours of a lover, and so keep their seed intact. They can be said to truly own themselves: other, promiscuous people are merely servants of their bodies rather than the possessors.*

> The summer's flower is to the summer sweet,
> Though to itself it only live and die,
> But if that flower with base infection meet,
> The basest weed outbraves his dignity:

*Even if the flower in summer does not propagate, it sweetens the summer by its very being. But if that flower meets with physical*

*disease, or contamination from inferiors, the most vulgar weed ha*
*more nobility and power.*

> For sweetest things turn sourest by their deeds;
> Lilies that fester smell far worse than weeds.

*For the most beautiful body can be corrupted by disease. If lilies*
*which we think of as chaste, become corrupt they will stink more tha*
*common plants.*

Shakespeare is trying to advise Southampton against liaison
with commonplace men like Edmones. As an aristocrat
Southampton has obligations of nobility. If these are not met
Southampton will destroy himself. This extraordinarily accurate
prophecy is echoed in Sonnet 69:

> They look into the beauty of thy mind,
> And that in guess they measure by thy deeds;
> Then, churls, their thoughts (although their eyes
>     were kind)
> To thy fair flower add the rank smell of weeds.
>     But why thy odour matcheth not thy show,
>     The soil is this, that thou dost common grow.

*Other people imagine what you are thinking – and judge that b*
*the things you do. Then they grow ungenerous – and though the*
*enjoyed gazing on your beauty as they would a lovely flower – think*
*you stink like a weed. But the real reason there is a dichotomy betwee*
*the way you look and the way you are is that you go to bed with an*
*Tom, Dick or Harry who takes your fancy.*

Shakespeare, fascinated that a young man can be beautiful
without and totally depraved within, explores this difference
between appearance and reality in much of his dramatic work.
As Duncan says in Macbeth: 'There's no art to find the mind's
construction in the face'. Shakespeare, in his own voice, says in
Sonnet 95:

Oh what a mansion have those vices got,
Which for their habitation chose out thee,
Where beauty's veil doth cover every blot,
And all things turn to fair that eyes can see!

*What a wonderful home depravity has found. You are so beautiful no-one can guess the darkness of your deeds – and imagine, because you look so good, you must be good.*

Take heed (dear heart) of this large privilege;
The hardest knife ill used doth lose his edge.

*Watch out! Even the best knife will become blunt if you abuse it.*

And in Sonnet 93:

For there can live no hatred in thine eye,
Therefore in that I cannot know thy change.
In many looks, the false heart's history
Is writ in moods and frowns and wrinkles strange;

*Your eyes never reveal your dark passions – so I can never tell what you have been up to. In a lot of people's faces, their past misdeeds register frankly in the set of their features.*

But heaven in thy creation did decree
That in thy face sweet love should ever dwell;
Whate'er thy thoughts or thy heart's workings be,
Thy looks should nothing thence but sweetness tell

*But Heaven, in creating you, ordered that only the workings of love should be seen in your face. Whatever you think about doing – or whatever you actually do – you keep the looks of an innocent.*

Shakespeare is building up a picture of a psychotic whose emotions and history do not register on his face. These observations are taken from life: but they eerily echo, down to the knife image, words written in 1578:

'We that are Christians ought little to esteem corporal beauty,

since that from it many times come great deformities to the soul
under the crystal ice is the dangerous mire: within the wrough
wall, is the cursed serpent nourished: within the white tooth doth
the importunate worm fret....within the beautiful body and face
of a pleasant countenance are horrible vices hidden. Although a
Nobleman may be very straight of body, of high lineage, well
shadowed with favours, very fair of beauty, very odoriferous
through fame, very high of blood...he for all this is not of better
life...Certainly a young man is like a blunt knife, the which in
tract of time is spoiled in the edge of the senses'.

The author? John Florio, translating Plutarch in his 'First
Fruits'.

●

Shakespeare himself was no angel. Every tour of actors
brings in its crop of infidelities and Shakespeare was no
exception. In Sonnet 110 he describes how he has 'gone here
and there' and made himself 'a motley to the view' by acting on
the stage and picking up casual lovers, making 'old offences of
affections new'. He admits he has lied about his activities to
Southampton, but, employing some of Berowne's special
pleading to justify his infidelity, claims:

> These blenches gave my heart another youth,
> And worse essays prov'd thee my best of love.

*My affairs made me feel young again. They proved to me that you
alone are my true love.*

In Sonnet 111 he blames his lack of money for his need to
work in the theatre – and blames 'the guilty Goddess' Fortune
for not providing 'better for' his 'life'. He has to rely on
'public means' – the box-office take – for his livelihood – and this
inevitably produces in him 'public manners' – a coarsened
sensibility.

Thence comes it that my name receives a brand,
And almost thence my nature is subdued
To what it works in, like the dyer's hand....

*My reputation is defamed; even my inner nature is tainted by
working in the theatre, like a dyer's hands, stained by his trade.*

In Sonnet 100, Shakespeare even attacks the very plays which
commercial pressure forces him to produce. His 'Muse' should
be concerning herself with 'that which gives (her) all (her)
might' – Harry Southampton himself. Instead she spends her
'fury on some worthless song' and so darkens her power 'to lend
base subjects light'.

Which of his plays, I wonder, did Shakespeare consider 'a
worthless song'?

●

In 1595 Southampton finally fell in love with a woman, the
Catholic Elizabeth Vernon, another of Elizabeth's jealously
guarded Ladies-in-Waiting. The Titchfield tradition is that
Shakespeare wrote 'Romeo and Juliet' in acknowledgement of
this passion, and though it comes too late to be written in
residence, Shakespeare certainly had the Southamptons – and
indeed the Montagues – in mind. The warring of the servants at
the beginning of the play mirrors the real life wars between the
servants of the 2nd Earl and Lord Montague when Mary
Southampton, accused of adultery, was denied access to
Titchfield. Even the balcony scene has a coded reference to the
Queen's jealousy of Elizabeth's beauty:

Arise fair sun and kill the envious moon [Elizabeth]
Who is already sick and pale with grief
That thou her maid art far more fair than she.
(Act 2, Scene 2)

Juliet's rage at Romeo, when she learns he has accidentally

killed Tybalt, is identical to Shakespeare's rages at Harry:

> O serpent heart, hid with a flowering face.
> Did ever dragon keep so fair a cave?
> Beautiful tyrant, fiend angelical,
> Dove-feathered'd raven, wolvish-ravening lamb!
>
> (Act 3, Scene 2)

It is the relationship between Mercutio and Romeo that most suggests Shakespeare's relationship with Southampton at Titchfield. Mercutio, sleeping in a truckle bed, keeps Romeo amused, much as Shakespeare did Southampton. Mercutio is also jealous of Romeo's love for Juliet – as Shakespeare must have been of Harry's love for Elizabeth. Shakespeare kills off Mercutio in an attempt to kill off what he hates in himself.*

In 1598 Elizabeth Vernon fell pregnant. Essex, in an attempt to get the knot tied before Queen Elizabeth could intervene, arranged a clandestine marriage at Essex House in August. Shakespeare, it seems, was not invited to this exclusive, aristocratic, crypto-Catholic ceremony. Southampton, like many gay men who suddenly go straight, was denying his past. He withdraws his love from Shakespeare. Sonnet 116 was Shakespeare's response to these events:

> Let me not to the marriage of true minds
> Admit impediments; love is not love
> Which alters when it alteration finds,
> Or bends with the remover to remove.

*You have been married – and at the service the priest has asked if there are any just causes or impediments why the service should not go ahead. But Harry, you and I have a spiritual affinity – and though*

---

* John Dryden wrote: 'Shakespeare showed the best of his skill in his Mercutio, and he said himself, that he was forced to kill him in the third Act, to prevent being killed by him.' *Essay on the Dramatic Poetry of the Last Age*, (1672). Dryden, unaware of the sub-text, finds this statement completely mystifying.

*ou have changed your attitude to me and withdrawn your love – I*
*jould not truly love you if I changed also and withdrew my love from*
*ou.*

> O no, it is an ever fixed mark,
> That looks on tempests and is never shaken;
> It is the star to ever wand'ring bark,
> Whose worth's unknown, although his height be
> taken.

*True love is like is like a beacon, undamaged by storms, for ships*
*oming home. It is like a guiding star: you can set your compass by it,*
*ut you will never really understand its true significance.*

> Love's not Time's fool, though rosy lips and cheeks
> Within his bending sickle's compass come;
> Love alters not with his brief hours and weeks,
> But bears it out even to the edge of doom.

*Love refuses to capitulate to Time, though beauty, even like yours*
*nd your new wife's, has no choice. Love stays entrenched till the Day*
*f Judgement.*

> If this be error and upon me proved,
> I never writ, nor no man ever loved.

*If I am mistaken, then all I have written is worthless. And all love*
*a delusion.*

In 'Henry IV Part Two' Prince Hal is crowned Henry V. His
old drinking companion, mentor and friend, Falstaff, certain of
advancement, waits to greet him outside Westminster Abbey: but
his affectionate cries of 'my royal Hal', 'my sweet boy' and 'my
heart' are met with a chilling response:

> I know thee not, old man: fall to thy prayers;
> How ill white hairs become a fool and jester.
>                               (Act 5, Scene 5)

Shakespeare, I believe, is dramatising his own rejection,

outside another 'church' at another time. But he now has th
emotional resource not to respond in kind. Moving with an eas
from the physical to the spiritual, he promises to lov
Southampton for all eternity. What had happened to him t
allow this generosity of response?

Two years earlier his son Hamnet had died, at the age o
eleven. Ben Jonson, responding to his own son's death, wrot
one of his most moving poems in which he described his boy a
'his best piece of work'. Shakespeare, typically, dramatised hi
grief in the words of Constance in 'King John', words that mus
go straight to the heart of any bereaved parent:

> Grief fills the room up of my absent child,
> Lies in his bed, walks up and down with me,
> Puts on his pretty looks, repeats his words,
> Remembers me of all his gracious parts,
> Stuffs out his vacant garments with his form
> 
> (Act 3, Scene 4)

But Shakespeare was also dramatising his own wife's grief.
believe this loss of their son brought some reconciliatior
between Shakespeare and Anne – and a need in Shakespeare to
enjoy the company of his surviving daughters. He had beer
seduced by the 'glamour' of the aristocracy and the theatre. Now
he could understand the true worth of 'ordinary' life – anc
purchased a Stratford home the following year. Davenant
claimed that Southampton gave Shakespeare £1,000 for 'a
purchase': if the story is true, it could well have been New Place

Sonnet 145 plays on Anne Hathaway's name ('I 'hate' from
'hate' away [Hathaway] she threw'). With its simple four beat
lines, it is often taken to be an early love poem from the teenage
Shakespeare:

Those lips that Love's own hand did make
Breath'd forth the sound that said 'I hate',
To me that languished for her sake;

But, as we have seen in 'A Midsummer Night's Dream',
Shakespeare, at thirty, employed the same 'rustic' form to
tremendous effect. Oberon squeezing love-juice on Titania's
eyes, proclaims:

What thou seest when thou dost wake
Do it for thy true love take;
Love and languish for his sake
(Act 2, Scene 2)

Shakespeare's sonnet continues:

But when she saw my woeful state,
Straight in her heart did mercy come,
Chiding that tongue that ever sweet
Was used in [used to] giving gentle doom, [judgement]
And taught it thus anew to greet:
'I hate' she altered with an end
That followed it as gentle day
Doth follow night, who like a fiend
From heaven to hell is flown away.
'I hate' from 'hate' away she threw,
And saved my life, saying 'not you'.

I believe this Sonnet is a product of Shakespeare's maturity –
written in a deliberately 'honest plain' way to his generous,
kind-hearted and forgiving 'country wife'. Having suffered the
roller-coaster ride of liaisons with Emilia and Harry, and brought
up against brutal reality by the death of his son, Shakespeare
truly 'languished' for the family life that circumstances had
denied him. It is significant that two months after Hamnet died
the Shakespeare family was granted a coat of arms. John
Shakespeare, claiming that an ancestor had been honoured by

Henry VII, had applied for one, unsuccessfully, in 1568. Now William added his weight to the application, both to please his father and to honour his own, grief-stricken family. Anne had much to hate in her faithless, distant husband. Shakespeare in this sonnet celebrates her forgiveness – and finally understands her worth.

A return to his family really had saved his life. His older daughter, Susanna, who was to inherit the bulk of his estate, was now a teenager. We know from 'King Lear' and 'The Tempest' how important, and sometimes difficult, the father-daughter relationship was to Shakespeare. Perhaps, in giving an unconditional love to her father, Susanna taught Shakespeare how to truly love Southampton.

The two men had experienced bitter fights, and there is a lot of door-slamming in the Sonnets on Shakespeare's part as well: 'Farewell, thou art too dear for my possessing' is the uncompromising opening of Sonnet 87. And, measuring Southampton's suffering by his own, in Sonnet 120 he can write, grimly, 'you've passed a hell of time'.

But he did keep his promise to Harry.*

---

* The bitter Sonnet 126 (in which Shakespeare reminds the 'lovely boy' that, however triumphantly he keeps his good looks, he must finally die) ends the sequence to Southampton. Many have read into this a disruption of the relationship. But this poem of twelve lines is not a sonnet at all – and I believe it was placed at the end because it is an oddity. Brackets indicate the original compositors thought the poem was incomplete – and Shakespeare, I hope to show, was still writing to Southampton at a time when he could no longer be considered, even by Shakespeare, as a 'boy'.

# CHAPTER 17.

# GREEN GEESE A-BREEDING

In 'Henry V' Shakespeare's Chorus asks the audience to imagine King Henry's triumphant return to London after Agincourt:

> But now behold,
> In the quick forge and working-house of thought,
> How London doth pour out her citizens

He compares this to the expected return of Essex from the campaign in Ireland – and the rapturous reception he will enjoy from the London public:

> As, by a lower but by loving likelihood,
> Were now the general of our gracious Empress,
>    [Elizabeth]
> As in good time he may, from Ireland coming,
> Bringing rebellion broached on his sword,
> How many would the peaceful city quit
> To welcome him!

>                    (Chorus, Act 5)

In 1599 Elizabeth sent Essex to Ireland to put down a rebellion. He failed. What is worse, he defied Elizabeth by appointing Southampton his Captain of Horse.

The two men had fought gallantly, but, provoked to distraction by the Queen who accused them of 'going on a Progress' in Ireland, they conceived a mad plan to overthrow and replace her with James VI of Scotland. On the eve of the Rebellion some of Essex's men paid the actors at the Globe to put on 'Richard II'. The intention was to stir the mobs to action by its depiction of Richard's abdication. It failed. Essex was beheaded and Southampton, his death sentence commuted, was imprisoned in the Tower. Typically, it was Mary Southampton who saved her son from death in a magnificent letter to Cecil:

'God of heaven knows I can scarce hold my hand steady to write and less hold steady in my heart how to write, only for what I know, which is to pray mercy to my miserable son. Good Mr. Secretary, let the bitter passion of a perplexed mother move you to plead for her only son for whom, if he had led the dance of this disloyalty, I protest to God I would never sue…'

Mary Southampton should have been a playwright as well.

What was Shakespeare's role in all this? Elizabeth thought Shakespeare was attacking her personally in 'Richard II': 'I am Richard II. Know ye not that?', she famously said. But it is one thing to write a play about an historical event, quite another to try to dethrone the Queen of England.

If Shakespeare did not join in the Rebellion, and if he had nothing to do with the performance of 'Richard II' (he was not named in the inquiry) how could he have remained a friend of Southampton? The clue can be found in the conclusion to Sonnet 70:

> Yet this thy praise cannot be so thy praise,
> To tie up envy, evermore enlarged,
> If some suspect of ill masked not thy show,
> Then thou alone kingdoms of hearts shouldst owe.

*Although I praise you, this praise is insufficient to prevent people becoming more and more jealous of you. People do not trust you – and so will never be loyal to you as subjects are to a King.*

Shakespeare knew that people would not follow Southampton, and is telling him so. I believe he also warned him that the Rebellion would fail. Southampton, languishing in prison, with Essex dead, would have finally seen the wisdom of his friend's advice.

Shakespeare knew that Essex, though popular with the people, was way out of his depth in the political world. This explains one of the greatest puzzles of 'Love's Labour's Lost' – the riddle of the Fox the Ape and the Humble-Bee.

In the play Costard trips over the threshold of the prison door and hurts his shin. Don Armado mentions a 'l'envoy' and Costard thinks he means a salve to heal his leg. Don Armado explains that 'l'envoy' is 'an epilogue or discourse to make plain/Some obscure precedence that hath tofore been sain.' Don Armado 'examples' it:

> The Fox, the Ape, and the Humble-Bee,
> Were still at odds being but three.

There's the moral: now the l'envoy.

Moth says he will add his own 'l'envoy':

> Until the Goose came out of door
> And stayed the odds by adding four.

Who is the Fox, who is the Ape, who is the Humble-Bee? And who is the Goose who comes out of door?

At the trial of Essex and Southampton, Sir Walter Raleigh was one of the main witnesses for the Crown. When he was sworn in, the Earl of Essex remarked that Raleigh should be made to place his hand on a large Folio Bible, rather than a small Testament, to show how much he was lying. Laughing, he added: 'What booteth it to swear the Fox?'. 'The Fox', clearly, was Essex's nick-name for Raleigh.

Who is the Ape? In 1607 Richard Nichols wrote a poem (published anonymously in 1627) called 'The Beggar's Ape'. One passage runs:

> But say, (Sir Ape) what wind brings you to court?
> Seems you have lived in some barren place

And want life's needments [necessities] for to do you
  grace;
That scarce your legs your limbs upholden can.

Most scholars take the Ape to be Sir Robert Cecil. I believe
Sir Robert was Shakespeare's Ape as well. He also appeared at
the trial, literally from the woodwork where he had been hiding,
to contradict the testimony of Essex who had asserted that Cecil
wanted the Infanta of Spain to be made Queen of England.

But what about 'the Humble-Bee'? In Sonnet 98
Shakespeare describes how in Springtime 'proud pied April
dressed in all his trim' puts 'a spirit of youth in every thing' – so
that even 'heavy Saturn laughed and leapt with him'. 'Old
Saturnus' was Essex's nick-name for Lord Burghley.*
Shakespeare is showing that the Spring is so powerful it can even
get that pompous old person leaping into the air.

One the most arrogant men in England, Burghley was also
the 'Humble B' of 'Love's Labour's Lost'. Shakespeare plays
further on the initial letter of Burghley's name when Katharine,
mocking Rosaline's dark skin, says she is 'Fair as a text B in a
copy book.' 'B' could well have been the Southamptons' name
for the grim-faced Burghley.

Burghley and Sir Robert would be well known to the
Titchfield audience. Both had attended the Privy Council
meeting there the September before. On 14th May, 1592, my
proposed date of 'Love's Labour's Lost', they were both safely
away, with Lord Hunsdon, at the Greenwich Privy Council
meeting. Raleigh, Cecil and his father Burghley were the three
men who contended most for power at the time of the play's
writing. Even Cecil enlisted Raleigh's help to appropriate some
of his father's estates.

---

* Paul E.J. Hammer, *The Polarisation of Elizabethan Politics* (1999)

But who is 'the Goose who came out of door/And stayed the odds by adding four'?

I believe it was the Earl of Essex. In the weeks before the performance of 'Love's Labour's Lost' Essex had been trying to reconcile his old enemy Raleigh with the Queen. Shakespeare was trying to warn Essex that he was indeed a silly 'goose' to meddle with the likes of Raleigh, Burghley and Cecil. He would end up on a spit like all the other geese at this Whitsun Fair.

Dover Wilson in 'The Essential Shakespeare', (1933) goes so far as to suggest that many of Shakespeare's plays are a covert dialogue with Essex. This is certainly suggested in an extraordinary letter written by Raleigh to Sir Robert Cecil (6 July, 1597 from Weymouth) in which he states that Essex 'was also wonderfully merry at the conceit of Richard the 2. I hope it shall never alter, and where I shall be most glad of, as the true way to all our good, quiet and advancement, and most of all for her sake whose affairs shall thereby find better progression.' Raleigh and Cecil encouraged Essex to identify with the brisk, dashing Bolingbroke who dethrones the corruptly incompetent, if beautifully articulate, 'Richard II'. They wanted Essex to attack Elizabeth so, eyes open at last, she would execute her favourite and put complete power into the hands of the Ape and the Fox.

But Shakespeare was ultimately to blame. He had used the theatre to work out all his frustration with Elizabeth by portraying her as the narcissistic, favourite-advancing Richard and fantasising about her deposition by 'Bolingbroke' – Essex in fancy dress. As the Gardener, the source of wisdom in the play, says of the King:

> The weeds that his broad-spreading leaves did shelter,
> That seem'd in eating him to hold him up,
> Are pluck'd up root and all by Bolingbroke –
> I mean the Earl of Wilstshire, Bushy, Green.
>
> (Act 3, Scene 4)

What the Gardener really means is Burghley, Raleigh and Cecil.

Ben Jonson praises Shakespeare for his 'brave notions'* Unfortunately Essex and Southampton – like the seducer in 'The Lover's Complaint' who would 'turn white and swoon at tragic shows' - took this particular brave notion literally. To Shakespeare's guilty horror, they stage the play at the Globe on Saturday, 7th February, 1601. The next day they act it out in life.

Shakespeare had earlier tried to give practical, political advice to the two men in Sonnet 25:

> Great Princes' favourites their fair leaves spread
> But as the marigold at the sun's eye
> And in themselves their pride lies buried,
> For at a frown they in their glory die.

*Elizabeth's favourite courtiers – beautifully dressed at the Queen's expense – are really just like marigold flowers that turn and face the sun – and their power and glory dies with them when they fall out of Elisa's capricious favour.*

> The painful warrior famoused for worth,
> After a thousand victories once foiled,
> Is from the book of honour razed quite,
> And all the rest forgot for which he toiled.

*Even a great, honest soldier – with scars to prove his valour – can win a thousand wars. But if he makes one political mistake, he is air-brushed out of history – and everything he lived and died for completely forgotten.*

The marigold image suggests the orange Devereaux armour that both Essex and Southampton wore.

By Sonnet 125, the time for advice is over. Essex has made

---

* In *Timber: or Discoveries; Made upon Men and Matter* (1623)

an unlicensed return to England from Ireland in 1599 – and has charged, covered with mud, into Elizabeth's morning bedroom at Nonesuch Palace. He has seen the old Queen in a shift with her 'hair down': for this she would never forgive him. She started by stripping him of his patent on sweet wines, his major source of income, and ended by chopping off his head. Shakespeare observes:

> Have I not seen dwellers on form and favour
> Lose all, and more by paying too much rent
> For compound sweet forgoing simple savour,
> Pitiful thrivers in their gazing spent?

*I have seen men who owed their very existence to their good looks and the Queen's patronage lose their money and their lives by giving up their very essence to Elizabeth. In order to gain a patent on sweet wines, one of the Queen's greatest gifts, they give up the simple gift of life itself. They flourish for a bit – but we must finally pity them. They have gazed upon the true form of their unadorned Queen – and so they die.*

When Shakespeare wrote these lines Essex was dead.

One of Shakespeare's greatest, and most mysterious, poems is 'The Phoenix and the Turtle'. This poem mourns the metaphorical 'death' of two chaste lovers:

> Death is now the Phoenix' nest
> And the Turtle's loyal breast
> To Eternity doth rest,
>
> Leaving no posterity:
> 'Twas not their infirmity,
> It was married chastity...

(Threnos. ll. 56-61)

Queen Elizabeth always presented herself as a phoenix – giving her own blood to succour 'Great Britain'. Is Shakespeare suggesting that Essex has achieved an equal dignity in death? Has the goose of the Titchfield Whitsun Fair finally transformed into a turtle dove?

●

During Southampton's imprisonment, Shakespeare went through suicidal despair. In Sonnet 66 he cries out for 'restful death' when he sees 'a beggar born' shunned by everyone while 'needy nothing', a man who has everything, is 'trimmed with jollity' - given even more. He has seen -

> purest faith unhappily forsworn
> And gilded honour shamefully misplaced

*To see Catholicism – with its roots back to the very beginnings of Christianity – apostatised: and titles and honours given to men disgracefully unworthy of them.*

> And maiden virtue rudely strumpeted,
> And right perfection wrongfully disgraced,
> And strength by limping sway disabl'd,
> And art made tongue-tied by authority,

*To see 'virginity' misused as a political weapon – and the men who cultivated their abilities to the highest peak unjustly made to suffer shame. To see young, strong men held back by older, feeble people in positions of power – and art strangulated by State censorship.*

> And folly, doctor-like, controlling skill,
> And simple truth miscalled simplicity,
> And captive good attending captain ill:

*To see stupid men, honoured by the establishment with degrees and status, holding back the truly talented; plain, straightforward dealing dismissed as stupidity and worthwhile people imprisoned and forced to serve worthless ones.*

> Tir'd with all these, from these would I be gone,
> Save that to die, I leave my love alone.

*Sick to death with these circumstances I want out. But if I did kill myself, I would leave my love to suffer by himself.*

Shakespeare and Southampton had, from boyhood, shared a 'purest faith' which both had to foreswear to survive. It is Southampton's 'strength' that is disabled by 'limping sway' (both Raleigh and Elizabeth walked with the aid of sticks). The 'simple truth' that Shakespeare has sought both in his work and his life is now thought of, in these cynical times, as stupidity. All of Southampton's goodness is 'captive': he has even been stripped of his Earldom. Shakespeare will not kill himself because it would leave Southampton 'alone', incarcerated in the Tower of London. Mary Southampton was allowed to visit her son in prison. It was she who acted as willing postman for the sonnets from Harry's loyal friend.

With the Accession of King James VI and I in 1603, the world seemed to brighten. Southampton was pardoned and released from the Tower – and Shakespeare celebrates the event in Sonnet 107:

> Not mine own fears, nor the prophetic soul
> Of the wide world, dreaming on things to come,
> Can yet the lease of my true love control,
> Supposed as forfeit to a confin'd doom.

*Neither my personal fears – nor the prophetic wisdom of the deep world's soul that knows all that is going to happen – can have any more influence on you, Harry, my true love, whom everyone thought had been imprisoned for life.*

> The mortal Moon hath her eclipse endur'd,
> And the sad augurs mock their own presage;
> Uncertainties now crown themselves assur'd,
> And peace proclaims Olives of endless age.

*Elizabeth is dead – the moon has proved mortal after all – and those who prophesied disaster at the end of her reign now laugh at their own gloomy prognostications. With the Coronation of James, everything is now secure – and his policies all point to 'peace in our time' and beyond.*

Shakespeare, who was attacked by Chettle, his former advocate, for not mourning Elizabeth's death,[*] has another dig at the dead Queen in his concluding couplet:

> And thou [Harry] in this [my poem] shall find thy monument,
>
> When tyrant's crests and tombs of brass are spent.

Elizabeth's refusal to name a successor had given rise to fears of a Spanish succession. Now James was on the throne, Catholics were hopeful part of the olive branch would come their way from the son of Mary Queen of Scots...

---

[*] 'Nor doth the silver tongued Melicert
Drop from his honeyed Muse one sable tear
To mourn her death that graced his desert
And to his lays opened her Royal Ear'. Henry Chettle, *England's Mourning Garment,* (1603)

# CHAPTER 18

# LIVING FOR CRIME

Hopes were soon dashed. James proved no friend to Catholics and Cecil exploited the Gunpowder Plot to discredit English Catholicism for centuries.*

What faith Shakespeare had left disappears almost completely in his great Tragedies. Although love sometimes survives, and the notion of the soul is not entirely lost, the universe seems at best indifferent, at worst, in league with malevolence. In the magnificent, unfinished 'Timon of Athens' a wish for death is presented as the only sane response to the selfish pointlessness of existence.

But Shakespeare still believes in selfless, plain-speaking, male friendship. Horatio will voice his misgivings to Hamlet and Kent will openly insult King Lear. Enobarbus, Antony's close friend and grizzled mentor, actually dies of grief when he abandons his Captain's hopeless campaign against Octavius. Shakespeare seems to be confessing his own guilt that he was not upon the barricades with Essex and Southampton. And that the 'fine frenzy' of his playwright's imagination had inspired them to the Rebellion. But earlier Enobarbus says:

> he that can endure
> To follow with allegiance a fallen lord
> Does conquer him that did his master conquer,
> And earns a place i'th' story.
>
> (Act 3, Scene 11)

* David Herber makes the point that Guido (Guy) Fawkes worked as a footman for the 2nd Viscount, Lord Montague at Cowdray. *Britannia.com LLC.* (1999). Fawkes came to the area just as Shakespeare was leaving it – Summer/Autumn 1592.

I believe Shakespeare did earn that place.

In his Late Plays, he finally regains something of his faith. Perhaps a return to the Church was the only possible alternative to madness or suicide. In 'The Winter's Tale' Paulina becomes the equivalent of the Catholic Priest, supervising Leontes' penance, remorse and redemption after he has wrongly accused his wife, Hermione, of adultery. Both husband and wife appeal to, and accept, the absolute authority – like Rome – of the Delphic oracle. When the 'statue' of Hermione is revealed in the chapel, she is 'adored' by Perdita, her long-lost daughter, who declares:

> do not say 'tis superstition, that
> I kneel and then implore her blessing.

Paulina warns Leontes:

> It is requir'd
> You do awake your faith. Then, all stand still;
> Or those that think it is unlawful business
> I am about, let them depart.

> (Act 5, Scene 3)

She then commands Hermione to 'descend'. As the statue comes to life, like so many Madonnas in Catholic tradition, the Virgin Mary seems to be returning to the land that has abandoned her. In 'Cymbeline', too, Shakespeare creates an absolute authority in Jupiter. The play ends with a Soothsayer prophesying a complete unification of Britain with Rome when 'our princely eagle,/Th' imperial Caesar' will 'unite/His favour with the radiant Cymbeline,/Which shines here in the west'. (Act 5, Scene 5).

More personally, Shakespeare deals with gay love in the play. The two sons of King Cymbeline, brought up in the wilds, not knowing their parentage, fall in love with the beautiful 'youth', Fidele, who turns out to be Imogen, their sister. Their instinctive love for a member of their own sex is sanctified by the resolution of the play and the link with Rome. In 'Henry VIII' Shakespeare comes out of the Papist closet completely. The saintly Katharine of Arragon makes her appeal directly to the Pope himself.

Prospero's last plea to the audience in 'The Tempest' is to be granted 'indulgence' – like a Papal indulgence – for his sins:

> Now I want [lack]
> Spirits to enforce, art to enchant;
> And my ending is despair,
> Unless I be reliev'd by prayer,
> Which pierces so that it assaults
> Mercy itself and frees all faults.
> As you from crimes would pardon'd be,
> Let your indulgence set me free.

*I have no more spirits to enact my will, or theatre to enthral an audience. At the ending of this play – and of my life – I have no hope at all unless I am pardoned by prayer – prayer which is so powerful a force that it can unlock the gates of mercy and free me from all sins. As you yourself seek to be forgiven, grant me the indulgence of your loving applause.*

Three years before his death in 1616 at 53, Shakespeare bought his only London property, the Blackfriars Gatehouse, famous for its recusant history and associations with the Gunpowder Plot, with its 'secret vaults and corners' and 'secret passages towards the water'. Having, in 'The Tempest' abjured the 'rough magic' of the theatre, which he never really liked and whose 'so potent art' had killed Essex and nearly killed Southampton, Shakespeare may well have re-entered 'real life', where 'every third thought' would be his 'grave', as an active

Catholic.* Certainly his beloved daughter, Susanna, got into trouble for failing to attend the Anglican Communion at Easter, 1607.

Shakespeare was certainly working on his soul in his last years. Sonnet 146 is actually a prayer in which Shakespeare condemns the attention he has given his body, which, from the looks of the Stratford-upon-Avon monument, had grown rather plump. Anticipating Donne, the sonnet concludes:

> Then soul, live thou upon thy servant's loss,
> And let that pine to aggravate thy store;
> Buy terms divine in selling hours of dross:
> Within be fed, without be rich no more,
> So shalt thou feed on death, that feeds on men,
> And death once dead, there's no more dying then.

*So let my spiritual being feed upon my physical body: let that dwindle to allow my soul to grow. Gain a heavenly life by abandoning the earthly one. Feed my inner self rather than my outer. That way you can consume death rather than be consumed by it. And once you've killed death itself, you will be immortal.*

There is no reason to doubt the Protestant Divine, Richard Davies (1688-1708) when he notes that Shakespeare 'died a Papist'.

●

Southampton found some sweetness in life when James came to the throne. He was pardoned, his Earldom was restored. He was even made a Knight of the Garter and, as such, would have

---

* There was no tenant at the Gatehouse till 1616, the year of Shakespeare's death. His name was John Robinson, and E.K.Chambers suggests he 'might conceivably' be the brother of Edward who entered the English College at Rome. *William Shakespeare – A Study of Facts and Problems*, (1930).

borne the canopy over James in his Coronation Procession in 1604*.

Shakespeare, as a member of the newly formed 'King's Servants', was given four and a half yards of red cloth to celebrate this event. We do not know if he marched in the Coronation Procession: but it is certainly not an 'honour' Shakespeare needs. He has seen what happens to the truly great and good under a tyranny:

> Were't ought to me I bore the canopy,
> With my extern the outward honouring,
> Or laid great bases for eternity,
> Which proves more short than waste or ruining?
> (Sonnet 125)

*Do you think I would 'give a damn' about carrying the canopy over James – as you did as a Knight of the Garter? With what is only superficial in me giving honour to what is even more superficial in him? Or set up triumphal 'pyramids' for the Coronation Procession – which promise everything for all time, but are made of wood and will fall down, or be smashed down, in an instant?*

Shakespeare mentions these 'pyramids' (which we would call obelisks) two sonnets before in Sonnet 123:

> No! Time, thou shalt not boast that I do change;
> Thy pyramids, built up with newer might;
> To me are nothing novel, nothing strange,
> They are but dressings of a former sight:

*Time, you cannot ever say that I was fickle: even these triumphal obelisks – built with such new hope for James's Coronation – are nothing new or weird to me. I've seen them before, much better done.*

Shakespeare *had* seen them before. They are the four

---

* It had been delayed from 1603 because of the Plague.

beautiful, tall, strong, marble obelisks that surround the Southampton family tomb at St. Peter's, Titchfield, which really are 'bases for eternity'.

In Sonnet 124 Shakespeare declares his love for Harry was never 'political':

> If my dear love were but the child of state,
> It might for fortune's bastard, be unfathered,
> As subject to time's love, or to time's hate,
> Weeds among weeds, or flowers with flowers gathered.

*If my love were simply motivated by worldly wisdom, it would be like a bastard child whom I could disown or acknowledge, depending on circumstances. I could leave my love wild and uncared for, like weeds in a garden, if it were politically expedient – or celebrate it, like gathering a bouquet of flowers, if it were politically correct.*

> No, it was builded far from accident;
> It suffers not in smiling pomp, nor falls
> Under the blow of thralled discontent,
> Whereto th'inviting time our fashion calls:

*No. My love was built like the wise man's house in the Bible – on rock, not sand. It won't be compromised by the unctuous triumph of King James – nor will it be smashed down by the malcontents who have been imprisoned by the new King – even though there is every pressure on us to conform with the times in this way.*

> It fears not policy, that heretic,
> Which works on leases of short numbered hours,
> But all alone stands hugely politic,
> That it nor grows with heat, nor drowns with showers.
> To this I witness call the fools of time
> Which die for goodness, who have liv'd for crime.

*My love has no fear of irreligious political plans which are always only short-term: it is completely independent and massively wise –*

*politic' rather than 'political'. Heat (State favour) will not make it*
*grow like a flower. Showers (State disapproval) will not drown it. To*
*bear witness I call upon the 'fools of time' who die for the sake of*
*goodness — though the simple fact of being alive has made them*
*criminals.*

Shakespeare has proved his love, not by what he has said but
by what he has done. His love for Harry is now so vast that it has
achieved a wisdom of its own. It is monumental in its certainty,
unique in its fidelity, sublime in its truth. So assured is
Shakespeare of its pure acceptability to heaven that he calls on
the 'fools of time' to witness it - those Catholic martyrs, Wells
and Genings, whose crime was to be Catholic and alive, one
owning a Fool's coat, the other paraded in it. Shakespeare sees
them as 'holy fools', those highest of beings. Time, as ever, has
proved Shakespeare right. Both men, one old and one so very
young, were created Saints by Pope Paul VI in 1970, the year of
my Cambridge production of 'Love's Labour's Lost'.

And Southampton, I believe, returned the love. When he
came out of prison he put on a play at his London house.

Guess which one.

# CHAPTER 19.

# OUR BRAZEN TOMBS

If you visit St. Peter's Church at Titchfield, you can see th beautiful tomb of the Southamptons. As ever with this family nothing is quite as it seems.

Jane Southampton, crowned, her hands in prayer, lies in th position of prominence. To her right, and lower, lies he husband, long-fingered, chin thrust forward, his Order of th Garter round his neck. To her left lies her beloved son, clad from head to foot in armour, though he never fought a battle in hi life. Beneath him kneels an image of her grandson, Harry, as boy, praying for the soul of his father. This tableau, protected b those four mighty 'pyramids', presents an image of harmony But, like stormy families who strive to look happy in photographs, the tomb is a lie.

The 2nd Earl had left provision in his will for two tombs. On for his mother and father, and one for himself. This request wa intended as an eternal rebuke to his 'unfaithful' wife, Mary. Sh had other plans. The 2nd Earl died in 1581: it was not till 159 that Mary got round to enacting his 'wishes' – the same year tha Harry came of age and might have his own ideas. Mary commissioned the Johnson family of Southwark to provide one tomb, not two, to her own specifications. Beneath the effigy o her husband she inscribed:

'Here lies the body of the Right Honourable Henry Wriothesley, Baron of Titchfield and Earl of Southampton who took to wife Mary Browne, daughter of Sir Anthony Browne Viscount Montacute and the Lady Jane Ratclyfe his wife, one o the daughters of Robert Earl of Sussex by which Mary he had Henry Earl of Southampton now living…'

Gloriously true to form, Mary Southampton has hi-jacked her husband's tomb. She even contrived to be buried in the family crypt, preserved, like all the Southamptons, in the purest honey.

The tomb had clearly been a huge issue. In Sonnet 81 Shakespeare laments that 'The earth can yield me but a common grave' whereas Southampton 'entombed in men's eyes shall lie'. Shakespeare, in Sonnet 55, consoles himself that not even the 'marble, nor the gilded monuments/Of Princes shall outlive [his] powerful rhyme' and that Southampton, in Shakepeare's verse, 'shall shine more bright' than 'unswept stone, besmeared with sluttish time'. The irony, of course, is that Shakespeare does have his own bust in the Parish Church at Stratford-upon-Avon while Southampton himself is doomed to a perpetual, prayerful childhood.

The Stratford monument was executed in 1623 by the same firm that had built the Southampton tomb at Titchfield. I believe Southampton, in an act of love the year before his own death, gave his friend a memorial. The 3rd Earl, described by the Venetian Ambassador as 'one of the bravest and noblest of [England's] cavaliers', did not want Shakespeare to be remembered only as the greatest of writers. He wanted him to be remembered as the greatest of men.

# POSTLUDE

As I was finishing this study, I was told, by chance, of a medieval stone fireplace, probably taken from Titchfield Abbey at its Dissolution, which stood in a house near the Grammar School. The owners invited me in to what was possibly the schoolmaster's dwelling.

I saw what I had been told about, but could hardly believe. Chiselled into the lintel was an 'HW', the 'H' at one end and the 'W' at the other, both with the characteristic circles at the end of each stroke that Henry Wriothesley used when he signed his name.

It is said that when Captain Cook sailed into Sydney Harbour, the aborigines could not see his ship. Something like that happened to me. It was back in London, hours later, and going to bed, that I recalled there was another initial on the fireplace, chiselled with interlocking V's.

It was another, very different, W.

# BIBLIOGRAPHY

*Calendar of State Papers Domestic and Foreign, Calendar of Charter Rolls, Calendar of Patent Rolls, Acts of the Privy Council, Privy Council Register, Calendar of Venetian State Papers and Statutes of the Realm* Public Record Office, Kew.

*Wriothesley Papers,* Winchester Record Office

G.P.V. Akrigg  *Shakespeare and the Earl of Southampton* (Hamish Hamilton, 1968)

Jonathan Bate *The Genius of Shakespeare* (Picador, 1997)

Edward Berry *Shakespeare and the Hunt* (Cambridge University Press, 2001)

Eustace F. Bosanquet *English Printed Almanacs and Prognostications* London Bibliographical Society, 1917)

M.C. Bradbrook *The School of Night* (Cambridge University Press, 1936)

A.C. Bradley *Shakespearean Tragedy* (Macmillan and Co. Ltd., 1904)

A.C. Bradley *Oxford Lectures on Poetry* (Macmillan and Co. Ltd., 1909)

Fr. H. S. Bowden *The Religion of Shakespeare* (London: Burns and Oates, Ltd., 1899)

David Buisseret  *Henry IV* (George, Allen and Unwin, 1984)

Richard Challoner *Memoirs of Missionary Priests* (1741)

E.K. Chambers William Shakespeare: *A Study of Facts and Problems* (Oxford, 1930)

ed. John Chandler  *John Leland. Itinerary – Travels in Tudor England* Alan Sutton, 1993)

ed. G. E. Cockayne *The Complete Peerage* (The St. Catherine's Press, 1959)

George Coffin Taylor *Shakespeare's Debt to Montaigne* (Harvard University Press, 1925)

Eamon Duffy *The Stripping of the Altars* (Yale University Press, 1992) ed. Richard David *Love's Labour's Lost* (Arden Edition, Methuen 1951)

J. Dover Wilson *The Essential Shakespeare* (Cambridge University Press, 1933)

Katherine Duncan-Jones *Ungentle Shakespeare* (The Arden Shakespeare, 2001)

Katherine Duncan-Jones *Shakespeare's Sonnets* (The Arden Shakespeare, 1997)

Mark Eccles *Shakespeare in Warwickshire* (The University of Wisconsin Press; Madison, 1961)

W. L. Edgerton *Nicholas Udall* (Twayne's English Authors, New York, 1965)

Arthur B. Ferguson *The Chivalric Tradition in Renaissance England* (Folger Books, 1986)

John Forrest *The History of Morris Dancing 1458-1750* (James Clarke and Co. Ltd, 1999)

Paul E.J. Hammer *The Polarisation of Elizabethan Politics* (Cambridge University Press, 1999)

Brice Haris *The Beggar's Ape Postscript* (New York, 1936)

G. B. Harrison *Willobie his Avisa 1594* (The Bodley Head Ltd. 1926)

ed. Keith Hayward *The Titchfield Parish Register 1590-163* (Titchfield Historical Society, 1998)

Margaret Hogden *The Fairs of Elizabethan England* (1942)

Anthony Holden *William Shakespeare: his Life and Work* (Little Brown, 1999)

Park Honan *Shakespeare A Life* (Oxford University Press, 1998)

Ronald Hutton *The Stations of the Sun* (Oxford University Press 1996)

David Kerr Cameron *The English Fair* (Stroud Sutton, 1998)

ed. John Kerrigan *The Sonnets and A Lover's Complaint* (Penguin Books Ltd., 1986)

G. Wilson Knight *The Wheel of Fire* (Oxford University Press, 1930)

Robert Lacey *Sir Walter Raleigh* (Weidenfeld and Nicolson, 1973)

David Lasocki with Roger Prior *The Bassanos* (Scolar Press, 1995) ed. Agnes Latham and Joyce Yovings *The Letters of Sir Walter Raleigh* University of Exeter Press, 1999)

ed. Sidney Lee *The Dictionary of National Biography* (London, Smith lder and Co., 1891)

Clara Longworth de Chambrun *Shakespeare Actor-Poet* (D. ppleton and Company, 1927)

Edmond Malone *The Life of William Shakespeare* (1821)

ed. Edmond Malone *The Plays and Poems of Shakespeare* (1821)

Judith M. Maltby *Prayer Book and People in Elizabethan and Early tuart England* (Cambridge University Press, 1998)

Gervase Markham *Honour in his Perfection* (1624)

Gervase Markham *The Gentleman's Academy* (1595)

Gervase Markham *Certain Excellent and New-Invented Knots* (1623)

Gervase Markham *Cavalry – or the English Horseman* (1607)

Michel de Montaigne *Essays translated by John Florio* (Everyman's library, 1921-46)

J. E. Neale *Queen Elizabeth I* (Jonathan Cape, 1934)

Charles Nicholl *A Cup of News – The Life of Thomas Nashe* Routledge and Kegan Paul, 1984)

John Nichols *The Progresses and Public Processions of Queen Elizabeth* 1823)

William Owen *The Book of Fairs* (1759)

ed. Pope and Warburton *The Works of Shakespeare* (1747)

R.R.Reid, *The Rebellion of the Earls, 1569* (Royal Historical Soc. Trans. Vol. XX, 1905)

A. L. Rowse *Shakespeare's Southampton* (Macmillan, 1965)

A. L. Rowse *The Poems of Shakespeare's Dark Lady* (Jonathan Cape, 978)

Eric Sams *The Real Shakespeare* (Yale University Press, 1995)

G. Scheurweghs *Nicholas Udall's 'Roister Doister'* (Louvain, 1939)

Samuel S. Schoenbaum *William Shakespeare. A Compact Documentary Life* (Oxford University Press, 1978)

William Shakespeare *Sonnets* (Scolar Press, 1968)

Charlotte Carmichael Stopes *The Life of Henry, Third Earl of Southampton* (Cambridge University Press, 1922)

Roy Strong *The Renaissance Garden in England* (Thames an Hudson, 1979)

Roy Strong *Gloriana. The Portraits of Queen Elizabeth I* (Thames an Hudson, 1987)

Dennis Taylor *Shakespeare and Religion in Post Reformation Englar* (www2.bc.edu/~taylor/shakes.html)

Raymond B. Waddington *The Mind's Empire – Myth and Form George Chapman* (John Hopkins University Press, 1974)

ed. George Watts *Titchfield, A History* (Polygraphic Ltd., 1982)

Evelyn Waugh *Edmund Campion* (Longmans, Green and Co., 193⁵

Glynne Wickham *A History of the Theatre* (Phaidon, 1985)

F.P. Wilson *The Plague in Shakespeare's London* (Oxford Universit Press, 1963)

Jean Wilson *Entertainments for Elizabeth I* (D.S. Brewer, Rowma and Littlefield, 1980)

Richard Wilson *Shakespeare and the Jesui* (www.lancs.ac.uk/users/english/jesuitp.htm)

ed. H.R. Woudhuysen *Love's Labour's Lost* (The Arden Shakespeare 1998)

Frances Yates *John Florio* (Cambridge University Press, 1934)

Frances Yates *A Study of Love's Labour's Lost* (Cambridge Universit Press, 1936)

Frances Yates *Astraea* (Routledge and Kegan Paul, 1975)

Alan Young *Tudor and Jacobean Tournaments* (George Philip, 1987)